Teaching Science in the Primary Classroom

Second edition

Hellen Ward, Judith Roden,
Claire Hewlett and Julie Foreman

Los Angeles • London • New Delhi • Singapore

First published 2005
Reprinted 2005, 2006(twice)
Second edition 2008

SAGE Publications Ltd
1 Oliver's Yard
55 City Road
London EC1Y 1SP

SAGE Publications Inc.
2455 Teller Road
Thousand Oaks, California 91320

SAGE Publications India Pvt Ltd
B 1/I 1 Mohan Cooperative Industrial Area
Mathura Road
New Delhi 110 044

SAGE Publications Asia-Pacific Pte Ltd
33 Pekin Street #02-01
Far East Square
Singapore 048763

Library of Congress Control Number 2008922906

British Library Cataloguing in Publication data

A catalogue record for this book is available from the British Library

ISBN 978-1-84787-376-7
ISBN 978-1-84787-377-4 (pbk)

Typeset by C&M Digitals (P) Ltd., Chennai, India
Printed and bound in Great Britain by TJ International Ltd, Padstow, Cornwall
Printed on paper from sustainable resources

Contents

Foreword

I'm delighted to welcome the second edition of this influential book on primary science. At last there is a book that clearly focuses on the promotion and development of science learning from the Foundation Stage to Key Stage 2. The four authors have extensive experience in initial teacher education and in primary schooling and this is evident in the emphasis on practical examples and evidence-based guidance.

Based in initial teacher education, the authors have based much of the content on recent and relevant research, with a particular aim of making the scientific content lively, contemporary and fun. This second edition has been extensively revised to include new developments in primary science and readings for each chapter.

Initial teacher education students, teachers and science leaders/co-ordinators in this country and overseas will find the book accessible, yet challenging. The examples and case studies are current and designed to help teachers make science learning active and creative. In the second edition the inclusion of more examples of children's work adds to the enjoyment and relevance of the book.

I believe that readers will welcome the assistance with planning, process skills and assessment, but more crucially will see how the range of components in the book contribute to science learning in the primary school.

Professor Hugh Lawlor
Director of AstraZeneca Science Teaching Trust
and Adviser to the Department for Children, Schools and Families (DCSF)

Acknowledgements

We would like to thank the many people who have contributed to this book, both directly and indirectly, including colleagues, both past and present, who have helped to shape the science courses upon which this book is based.

Thanks are due to the many ex-students and teachers, in the institutions in which we have worked, who have provided the inspiration and opportunities for us to develop our ideas about teaching science over the years. We would like to acknowledge the support provided by the AstraZeneca Science Teaching Trust with their funding for projects including the most recent personalised learning in science project, some of the work generated has been included in this second edition of the book.

In particular we would like to thank the Head teachers, teachers and children of the following schools:

All Souls Primary School, Dover, Kent
Bobbing Village School, Kent
Davidore Infant School, Brighton and Hove West Sussex
Elphinstone County Primary School Hastings East Sussex
Eythorne and Elvington Primary School, Kent
Graveney Primary School, Graveney, Kent
Hawkinge Primary School, Hawkinge, Kent
Herne Bay Infants School, Herne Bay, Kent
Hollington County Primary School, Hastings East Sussex
Iwade Primary School, Iwade, Kent
Joy Lane Primary School, Whitstable, Kent
Morehall Primary School, Folkestone, Kent
Park Wood Junior School Rainhan, Medway
Senacre Wood Primary School Maidstone, Kent
Skinner Street Primary School, Gillingham, Medway.
St Benedict's RC Primary School Chatham, Medway
St Mary's, Ashford, Kent
Whitfield and Aspen, Dover, Kent
Whitstable Junior School, Kent

More specifically, we owe many thanks to, Hugh Ritchie who has provided much encouragement and essential support during the preparation of this book. We are indebted to him for his work in producing many of the photographs included in the book. We would also like to thank Keith Remnant and Paddy Grinter for their skills in proof reading and editing.

About the Authors

Hellen Ward is actively involved in science education, working as a science senior lecturer at Canterbury Christ Church University and with teachers in a number of Local Authorities. Hellen has written several books and a number of other publications, and has developed teaching resources and teaching materials to support the teaching and learning of science. She has also contributed to science television programmes, website and teaching resources for the BBC and the teacher training resource bank (ttrb.ac.uk). Hellen is Programme Director for Modular PGCE at Christ Church and is also an independent education consultant. Hellen is an active member of the Association for Science Education (ASE). She is a regional secretary and a regular contributor to both national and regional conferences. She is also a member of the Association for Achievement and Improvement through Assessment (AIAA) and has published materials on assessment. Hellen is currently involved in a personalised learning project funded by AstraZeneca science teaching trust.

Judith Roden is an experienced teacher of science in all phases of education. She is currently a Principal Lecturer working in the Faculty of Education, Canterbury Christ Church University, where she undertakes the role of cross-phase science team leader, managing a large team of science tutors. She has written the *Reflective Reader in Primary Science Education*, co-wrote *Extending Knowledge in Practice* as well a number of articles and chapters in respected science books. Having run two successful projects in 2000 and 2001, Judith is now the project director of the University's new AstraZeneca Science Teaching Trust funded school-based project focusing on personalised learning in science with schools in Kent and Medway.

Claire Hewlett has many years' experience teaching in primary schools in East Kent. She spent five years as a science co-ordinator prior to becoming a headteacher. Claire is a Senior Lecturer in the primary education department and has worked on projects in Malaysia and India. She is currently involved in an AstraZeneca Science Teaching Trust personalised learning project with schools in Kent and Medway.

Julie Foreman is an experienced teacher of science in primary education. She is currently a Senior Lecturer working in the Faculty of Education at Canterbury Christ Church University, where her main area of work is primary science education, working with a range of students including undergraduates, postgraduates and specialist teacher assistants. Julie was involved with the University's AstraZeneca Science Teaching Trust-funded school-based project, from which she has undertaken research and conference presentations. Her further areas of research have focused upon children's investigative science and the use of role-play to stimulate and develop children's understanding of scientific concepts.

1

What is Science?

Judith Roden and Hellen Ward

Introduction

This chapter will explore the reasons why science is important for people of all ages and why it is a crucial element of an innovative, cross-curricular primary framework requiring a high profile in the primary school. The chapter will outline the nature of science and the development of scientific ideas. Drawing on recent research into learners' attitudes towards science, the focus will be on how creative science can be developed. Additionally, it will explore the importance of ideas and evidence, starting with learners' ideas and encouraging them to collect and interpret their own data thereby helping them to think and reason for themselves while developing a respect for evidence. These features will be interwoven to demonstrate that it is the development of learner attitudes towards science that impacts on their learning both in the short and long term.

Why Science Is Important

The prosperity of the United Kingdom (UK) since the Industrial Revolution of the nineteenth century arose out of the ideas, inventions and creativity of the artisans, scientists and technologists that facilitated the development of its heavy industrial base. While the creation and design of innovative new products is still of paramount importance, in the UK there has been an almost total move away from the heavy and light engineering and manufacturing base of the past. Instead, and increasingly, western developed countries depend highly for their income on service industries including the financial services and on highly specialised manufacturing industry. Typically, the trend now is for the mass manufacture of everyday products to take place in those parts of the world where labour costs are generally cheaper and where there is an enthusiasm for the adoption of western culture and affluence. Globally this has resulted in the rise of countries such as China and India as super-powers and their increasing importance on the world stage.

Today, although the 'dark satanic mills' of the past have been replaced by less obvious ways of wealth acquisition, there has never been such a recognition that science and its allied subjects are of fundamental importance:

> It is vital to our economy and to the country's prosperity that we maintain and develop our science base – we are committed to doing this. We need the right people with the right skills to build a strong science base and we are determined to ensure a good supply of scientists, engineers, technologists and mathematicians ... we have a responsibility to capture the imagination of young people who will become the scientists, technologists, engineers and mathematicians of the future, and to help them to reach their full potential. (The Science, Technology, Engineering and Mathematics (STEM) Programme Report (2006) Foreword, DfES/DTI)

However, the production of scientists is not the sole reason for the need for the development of science education in schools: 'Science and technology are essential ... to our quality of life, and lie at the heart of our history and culture' (Science and Technology Committee, 2002, Introduction, p.1).

In order to meet its responsibilities, an education system must address two major closely-linked needs: the needs of the individual and the needs of society. To succeed in the global economy, modern-day developed countries need their education systems to produce well-qualified scientists and technologists who will be the researchers of tomorrow. Simultaneously they must produce well-balanced, well-informed, scientifically literate adults who are adaptable, possessing a range of generic and specific skills, aptitudes and abilities that will enable them to take up the many and varied employment opportunities of today and in the future. Adaptability is important to individuals because they may need to be capable of changing their type of employment, perhaps repeatedly, to meet the challenges of a rapidly changing technological society.

Crucial to the future health of an economy and key to the success of its individuals is for all of its citizens to possess effective communication skills. Science has an important role in this process. At a time when learners spend their time passively, often alone, watching television, listening to music or playing computer games, school science provides the opportunity for discussion and the sharing of ideas so crucial for the development of communication skills. It is imperative, even more so than in the past, that such opportunities are provided at the primary level and developed systematically throughout the education system. Learners need to develop a sound understanding of science and the ability to consider scientific evidence objectively.

Scientific Literacy: the Public Understanding of Science

Historically, in the UK, there has been a gap in the understanding of science by different groups of people. While those interested in science have pursued science-related occupations and have become more specialist in the scientific knowledge they hold, the education system has allowed many others to reject science at an early stage. Unfortunately this has had two significant and undesirable outcomes. Firstly, many people, some would argue the vast majority, have rejected science and science-related activities, possibly because of the link with heavy industry. Secondly, scientists themselves have become so specialised in their own knowledge and understanding that a gulf has developed between the two significantly different groups in society.

Typically, there has been a general reluctance for many to 'do' science in the past, especially in 'elite' echelons of society. The education system in the nineteenth century prepared individuals to fit into their sections of the highly stratified class system:

> ... a functional perspective equated schooling with social status. In the propriety schools of the mid-nineteenth century a hierarchy of practical, commercial, and liberal, educational provision was matched to gradations within society ... the middle ranks in society still found educational opportunities too limited ... the established public schools ... felt their central function was to act as social agencies for transforming upper-class boys into English gentlemen ... By the second half of the nineteenth century it was not gentleman, but businessmen, scientists and skilled artisans for whom England had the greatest need. (Digby and Searby, 1981, pp.110–11)

Hence, science was often seen as inferior (ibid., p.34) and not recognised as important at any level in education. In particular 'public schools were sluggish in recognizing the need to provide scientific education for their upper-class clientele' (ibid., p.111). Indeed, even some who made their money out of successful industrial enterprise seemed to conspire in the process of devaluing the very skills, knowledge and understanding essential to industrial development in order to improve social standing:

> The wealthy manufacturer sends his son to classical school to learn Latin and Greek as a preparation for cloth manufacturing, calico printing, engineering or coal mining ... After his scholastic career he enters his father's factory absolutely untrained. (Roderick and Stephens, 1981, pp.238–9)

This scenario compounded the status of science among influential groups and some argue caused a downturn then in the national economy in England. Many, in the past and still today, have not recognised that science offers anything to their everyday lives, rejecting science because they consider it too difficult or irrelevant.

Even when science eventually increased in status and was introduced into a few universities, scientists themselves were few in number and formed an elite group. Even as late as 1884, Francis Galton concluded that 'an exhaustive list' of scientists in the British Isles 'would amount to 300, but not to more' (Khan and Sokoloff, 2007, p.12). Arguably, some would say, they failed to make a significant contribution to the development of the economy at that time:

> Despite the advantages that people from their class backgrounds had at invention, it must be noted that scientists were not all that well represented among the great British inventors until very late in the 19th Century ... Instead, the evidence regarding technical knowledge of all kinds comported more with ... James Nasmyth's definition of engineering as 'common sense applied to the use of materials' (ibid., p.13).

Clearly the gap between scientists and 'others' has a long and complicated history, but it helps to explain why perhaps there has been a traditional gap between these two groups in society. Consequently, in the nineteenth century, and as still can be evidenced today, these two groups sometimes fail to share a common vocabulary and find communication difficult.

Today, the above scenario is at best undesirable and at worse potentially disastrous. There is a very close link in a democratic society between the development of government thinking and the level of its citizens' understanding of science. Public opinion can be highly influential in determining government policy. In the early years of the twenty-first century in the United Kingdom there has been a definite move towards the adoption of a 'green' agenda by all the main political parties because of public pressure, whereas such ideas were restricted to those labelled as 'cranks' and 'liberals' in the 1970s. Change has come about not least through the discussion of related issues in the popular media.

Many modern-day issues, such as a proposed move to increase nuclear power for the production of electricity, or the siting of mobile phone masts or wind turbines, are contentious. Even different groups of scientists themselves may hold differing views on the same issue, for example, many environmentalists argue for alternative forms of energy such as wind farms, while ornithologists argue against them for totally different reasons.

Other issues raise ethical questions, such as the use of stem cells in medicine or the cloning of 'Dolly the Sheep'. However, if government decisions are to be based on evidence rather than on irrational fears and uninformed opinion, the voting population will need an understanding of science to enable them to make informed decisions about these and other important issues related to science in society; for example, genetically modified crops, global warming, etc. Even more importantly, perhaps, individual 'family' units need to be able to make sense of and understand the evidence relating to medical issues such as vaccinations and the possible links with health and disability, and other life choices related to diet and leisure.

Making sense of the evidence, however, when much of it appears contradictory, is far from easy, particularly when it is given a particular slant or 'spin' by politicians or when the presentation of ideas has been sensationalised or if complex issues have been over-simplified by the popular media that confusion and bewilderment results.

Administrations, if they are to endure, cannot afford to ignore public opinion, especially if there are economic consequences involved. Resulting from the concern about the effects of global warming linked with climate change, in 2006 the Labour government in England commissioned a very lengthy, independent review to examine critically the scientific and economic evidence for the theoretical impact of climate change around the world. The Stern Review Report on the Economics of Climate Change adopted a questioning stance and provided an in-depth examination of a considerable amount of evidence from different types of research from around the world. The review makes for interesting reading, particularly in its predictions for the movement of man and other animals as they adapt to the changes in local temperature as global warming takes effect over the world. The report concludes that the effects of climate change, arising from global warming are a direct result of man's impact on the global environment. The review is persuasive; it could be argued that Stern adopted a pessimistic stance towards the available evidence that was mainly drawn from theoretical models (Mendelsohn, 2006; Tol, 2006). Others have argued strongly that, while there are issues that need to be addressed within our society, global change and climate change are merely part of an inevitable pattern of climate change that has little to do with man's activities. Indeed, existing fossil records testify to the fact that significant and influential temperature variations on a global scale over time have occurred without man's influence. Although Stern briefly mentions that global climate change has occurred naturally in the past, the review emphasises the effects of CO_2 emissions resulting from man's activities today.

Regardless of whether man's activities are accelerating climate change and whether man can reverse those changes, there are environmental issues needing to be addressed as a matter of urgency, for example there is a need to curb the long historic practice of burying waste, particularly in our 'throw-away' society in the UK.

Many young people are concerned about the future of the planet and have been quick to adopt recycling practices. However, they may well be ignorant of the finer details of the issues for which they show enthusiastic support; some initiatives related to the environment may well be storing up problems for the future. One example here relates to the trend towards replacing traditional domestic light bulbs with a 'long-life' variety. Few stop to ask about the risks and hazards associated with this practice, yet there will be a need to deal with the disposal of the spent bulbs and the mercury that they contain at some point in the near future. The recycling of rubbish may also be questioned. There is a cost here, not often explored in terms of energy required for the collection of recycled rubbish, particularly if additional car journeys are made to take the rubbish to waste disposal points – especially in rural areas. The trend towards banning the sale of plastic carrier bags or charging highly for them may also yield unexpected consequences: people may drive to the supermarket and back rather than walking. Such problems are typical of those that our learners will need to consider and make informed decisions about in the future.

The Four Threads of Science

Historically, science has had two aspects: first, a body of knowledge and, second, a way of working. The two aspects are totally and inextricably linked. Whenever scientists work, they find out about the world using aspects of scientific method. Similarly, pre-school and older learners find out about the world using the same basic methods. Although the level of sophistication of the tasks will be different and the tools used also different, basically both scientists and learners find out about the world using the same processes. For many years, in theory, if not always in popular practice, one of the principal aims of science education has been to develop learners' understanding through the use of scientific approaches.

Being scientific also involves the development of concepts like electricity or change or movement, etc. There is a strong relationship between learners' use of scientific method and the development of scientific understanding. Furthermore, developments in both aspects of science are strongly influenced by, and rely upon, scientists' and learners' attitudes towards science. The atti-. tudes involved in 'being scientific' generally include curiosity, respect for evidence, willingness to tolerate uncertainty, creativity and inventiveness, open-mindedness, critical reflection, co-operation with others, sensitivity to living and non-living things and perseverance. Although Johnson (2005) sees scientific development as a 'triple helix' with three threads, conceptual understanding, skills and attitudes all developing together to support later understanding, a further area is important in joining the strands together: this is the area of scientific procedures.

Scientific procedures are different from skills and include the nature of science, the collection and consideration of evidence and the development of scientific ideas. Procedural understanding develops learners' understanding of the scientific approach to enquiry, so that they use these ideas in a scientific way.

These four threads are linked and are vital if science is to continue to have any relevance for learners in the twenty-first century. Without this breadth, science is a dry and limiting subject which fails to interest and excite, and where the past trials and successes are reduced to a list of facts to be learnt and experiments to be conducted.

The Importance of Science in the Primary School

Recent change in science at secondary level has reflected a recognition that significant change in practice was needed to ensure that future citizens become scientifically literate. Since May 2006 Key Stage 4 courses in science have emphasised the notion of 'how science works'. The change has come about because of a long-held belief that the science curriculum was overloaded with 'facts to be learnt'. Since 2007 science at Key Stage 3 has become focused around key concepts, key processes, range and content and curriculum opportunities. The content statements have been reduced to four areas of science with life processes becoming part of organism behaviour and health. There has been no change in the programme of study at Key Stages 1 and 2 since 2000 and the last real change occurred in 1995. As a result the primary curriculum is becoming out of step with science in other areas of education and science in real life. Science is a core subject in the National Curriculum that contributes to the acquisition of key skills, including thinking skills (Harlen, 2000a; 2000b).

The debate about what the emphasis of science should be has raged for many years. Science did not become accepted at school level until the late nineteenth century (Lawson and Silver, 1973, p.345). Even then, there was disagreement about what school science should consist of. Professor Henry E. Armstrong campaigned for a more 'enlightened' approach. He attacked (ibid., pp.345–6) existing teaching methods and advocated 'heuristic' or 'discovery' methods stating that 'boys and girls in the future must not be confined to desk studies: they must not only learn a good deal *about* things, they must also be taught how to *do* things … so that children from the outset may learn to acquire knowledge by their own efforts' (ibid., p.346). More recently, set in a context when teacher educators were trying to encourage primary teachers to include science in their classroom, Harlen (1978) questioned whether content mattered in primary science. Over a decade later, the launch of the Science National Curriculum at Key Stages 1 and 2 in 1989 saw the swing to the practice of a content-driven curriculum, even if this had not been the intention of the writers of what were to become the first statutory orders. Almost 20 years later the debate rages on.

Even with an increasing move towards a cross-curricular approach it is important that science features clearly and has a recognisable, discrete identity if learners are not to receive a diet of science lacking in depth and relevance. This fact has been understood for some time; however, it would be unfortunate if this understanding was now lost.

> The field of science is so wide that what is done in school can jump from one facet of the subject to another without much sense of cohesion developing … even when a topic for enquiry has been selected, the ramifications to which it can lead need to be kept under control, if a sense of definite accomplishment is to result. (Ministry of Education, 1963, p.143)

According to the National Curriculum (DfEE, 1999), science is about stimulating and exciting children's curiosity about the world around them: 'Science is an integral part of modern culture. It stretches the imagination and creativity of young people. Its challenges are quite enormous' (DfEE, 1999, p.78). Given this view, it is not surprising that the development of aspects of scientific skills can be identified in the Early Years Foundation Stage (DfES, 2003a) in the Curriculum Guidance for the Foundation Stage, within the aspect of 'Knowledge and Understanding of the World'. It is also promoted in both Key Stages 1 and 2 of the English National Curriculum. The Qualification and Curriculum Authority (QCA) (2000, p.32) states that in order for children in the Foundation Stage to successfully develop their knowledge and under-standing of the world, teachers need to provide: 'Activities based on first-hand experiences that encourage exploration, observation, problem solving, predic-tion, critical thinking, decision making and discussion' (QCA, 2000, p.82) – a real challenge for the early years practitioner and indeed all teachers and oth-ers who work in the classroom with learners of all ages!

Attitudes for learning science are also important and need consideration and development. Attitudes do not feature explicitly in the science National Curriculum 2000, however, they are important and, when considering a child's education holistically, cannot be ignored. Worryingly there seems to be a trend for learners to turn away from science as they get older, linked to the way that science concepts are revisited in preparation for National Tests at Key Stage 2.

Overall, the development of understanding of science is dependent on all these aspects. Teachers need to weave a carpet of provision of science for primary-aged children where knowledge and understanding develop alongside scientific procedures, skills and attitudes towards and in science.

Learners' Attitudes towards Science

Research into learners' attitudes towards science reveals that they are formed at an early age. Therefore, it is crucial to capture this natural interest in science and to capitalise upon learners' experiences of finding out about the world through exploration. The aim of school science is to extend these opportuni-ties, rather than to limit the curriculum, as seems to be the case today in some schools. The Acclaim Project (www.acclaimscientists.org.uk) interviewed emi-nent scientists engaged in current research and development in science. One of the most interesting findings related to the age at which scientists had first become interested in science. Typical responses included:

'I don't remember when I was not interested in science.'
'I was interested in science from a very young age, perhaps 5 or 6.'

While female scientists seemed to suggest they were older when their interest in science began, a common factor identified for all was the exposure to other people who had a passion for things scientific, such as a parent, relative or friend. Significantly, teachers and 'hands-on' experiences were both identified as factors that played an influential role in developing the scientists' interest in science. This concurs with views regularly expressed by practising and intending teachers whose own experiences in school science, both positive and negative, impact significantly on their long-term attitudes towards the subject.

Clearly, then, it is important for science to feature regularly throughout the primary years. However, it is important not only that it is included, but that it is of the right quality. Her Majesty's Inspectorate (HMI) subject report for Primary Science (Ofsted/HMI, 2003) found that there had been a reduction in the time given to science and, particularly, for investigative work.

Other research suggests that many learners have poor attitudes towards learning in science at the primary level. Pollard and Triggs (2000) found that as the learners in the sample grew older, science became one of three subjects least liked in the primary curriculum and that, by Year 5 and Year 6, learners rarely nominated science as the subject most liked, favouring art and physical education instead. Learners said they found science difficult and disliked both the amount of writing they had to do and the weight of information they had to learn. Girls consistently disliked science more than boys until Year 6 when antipathy was much more evenly divided between the sexes. Also the findings suggested that as primary learners grew older, their awareness of learning processes in science declined rather than grew. For example, there was a decline in their awareness of science as an investigative activity because of the tightly-framed subject-based and teacher-controlled curriculum (Pollard and Triggs, 2000, pp.87–98).

Learners need to be provided with both the opportunity and the time to engage with the processes and the procedures of science in order to develop sound knowledge and understanding, and to develop more positive attitudes as a result.

The Nature of Scientific Ideas

The range of accepted scientific knowledge and understanding is immense and has been developed over thousands of years. The body of known science knowledge, however, is not static and unchanging. The process of change happens gradually: many original ideas have been challenged over time, for example, the ideas that the earth is the centre of the universe and is flat. Other ideas have been refined over time, for example, the idea that the smallest parts of an atom are neutrons, electrons and protons. However, most of the ideas in science that are accepted as true today have one thing in common: although the ideas are not accepted absolutely, there is some evidence to support them. Although there is a commonly held idea that scientists set out to 'prove' their ideas, in reality, scientists set out to 'disprove' their ideas. An idea is adopted because conclusions have been drawn and have been communicated to others, which has resulted in the idea being challenged and either rejected or accepted. No matter how much evidence there is to support a theory, it takes only one repeated finding to disprove an idea. Sometimes change occurs through a process of a scientific revolution when accepted ideas are looked at in a new and novel way – when a scientist steps outside existing paradigms and takes a creative look at accepted ideas, this can lead to giant leaps in scientific understanding (Khun, 1962).

Learners need to develop an understanding of the ways in which previously accepted scientific facts have changed over time if they are really to appreciate the essential essence of science. This aspect of science should be explicitly included in the teaching and learning approaches used in the primary school, which should include some reference to science in the past. If not, science merely becomes a body of knowledge that has to be learnt, with no opportunities for

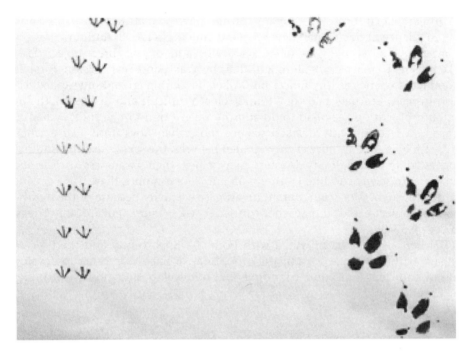

Figure 1.1   What ideas are generated by this picture?

'new' discoveries or a creative response on behalf of the learners. The focus on *what* is known, rather than *how* it is known, makes science sterile. Evaluating evidence is important in science and is also an important generic life skill. Open-mindedness and respect for evidence are important attitudes in science and important also in everyday life, i.e. making decisions based upon evidence rather than jumping to conclusions.

Enabling learners to make the link between their ideas and the evidence for them can be encouraged through simple activities. A good activity to make explicit the need to look objectively and to respect evidence to support con-clusions follows, starting with Figure 1.1.

Many ancient sets of footprints have been found and these have fascinated scientists for decades. Learners can be asked to reveal the ideas they hold as a result of looking at the picture above. When shown this drawing recently, some learners stated that they thought the drawings were of footprints. When asked why they thought this, it was clear that they had brought evidence from everyday life to their interpretation of the drawing, for example having seen birds' footprints in the snow. They also stated that one animal was bigger than the other, as evidenced by the size of the footprint, and that the animal with larger prints had claws. While the smaller animal moved with both feet together, the larger footprints were made one at a time. An adult learner suggested that the small footprints were made by an animal with a small brain who had not evolved a brain big enough to have co-ordinated movement.

Figure 1.2   More evidence is provided; have the ideas changed?

When more evidence (Figure 1.2) was presented, the learners put forward ideas of a meeting between the two animals, resulting in the smaller animal flying away, having a piggyback or coming to a 'sticky end'. The evidence that supported these ideas was elicited and questions were asked which focused the learners on what evidence explicitly supported their ideas and whether all ideas could be correct. In this case all ideas had merit, although learners developed their 'pet idea', but it was not possible to discount the other views. In fact, there was no evidence to suggest that both footprints were made at the same time! Once the learners realised that in this type of science lesson the expectation was for them to promote ideas, to discuss evidence and that their responses could be modified as more evidence came to light, they were ready and willing to use their enthusiasm and creativity in other activities. Challenging learners to use their ideas and collect evidence can occur in most activities, but it requires changes to the way that science is delivered in some primary classrooms.

Tracks in everyday modern life provide as many challenges as using examples from pre-history. The tracks in Figure 1.3 were made on a beach in the USA in

Figure 1.3   What made these tracks?

2004. Looking at the different tracks should provide some evidence as to the 'animals' that made them. Enabling learners to be creative just requires less teacher direction and an understanding that science can be meaningful. Making tracks at school to solve problems and include forensic science into classroom is discussed in chapter 5.

On another occasion, everyday materials were used to link science to real life. Learners were asked to apply this approach to an everyday setting situation. A range of cans of proprietary soft drinks, i.e. a 'Coke', a 'Diet Coke' and a 'Seven-up' and a tank of water were used to challenge learners to provide ideas of what would happen when the cans were placed in water. Learners used previous knowledge of floating and sinking to arrive at suggestions. These included 'Diet Coke will float as it is lighter' and 'They will all sink because they are heavy'. The cans were placed into the water one by one, with an opportunity for the learners to observe what happened to each can, and learners were asked if they would like to alter their ideas based on the new evidence. In the event, the 'Seven-up' sank, the 'Coke' floated just off the bottom and the 'Diet Coke' floated just below the surface, which resulted in amazement and quick suggestions as to why this might be. The learners then had to think of ways to test out their ideas.

Suggested tests included weighing the cans, measuring the liquid, counting the number of bubbles in set amounts of each liquid and the use of secondary sources to research the composition of each liquid (for example, amount of sugar). One child suggested that if the cans had been placed in the tank in a different order a different result would have occurred! Identifying learners who require support or challenge is an additional advantage of working in this way.

Although no writing was involved in the original part of the session, this did not make this activity less valuable. When the learners tried out their tests they recorded their results and communicated their findings in poster form later in the week.

Simple Starting Points for Interesting and Creative Activities

Initially, when asked to use a simple object as a starting point for creative science activities, practising teachers and students in training often state that they find this difficult and scary. However, when challenged to do so, they often provide a wealth of ideas for sharing with colleagues: 'At first I was really worried, I didn't know what I could choose, but when you think carefully, look in books and so on, it is so simple, isn't it!' (PGCE student, 2004).

Creative and interesting activities can be developed from many different, but simple starting points. Table 1.1 provides some suggestions for creative practical activities from starting points where the initial focus is on play, exploration and observation. Many of the activities can be approached at different key stages, but need to be tailored to meet the known needs of individuals and groups of learners in the classroom. Teachers and other adults can start by presenting the object to the child, stepping back to observe what learners notice, how they interact with the object(s) and noting what questions are asked. Differentiation is by outcome, as initially the learners will approach each task with differing levels of skills and experience. It is found that younger learners will approach objects in a different way to older learners, with their approach based on trial and error. The expectation of older learners is that they will apply a more systematic, logical approach to the activities, although this depends upon previous experiences and opportunities to work independently.

Table 1.1   Creative Practical activities

Resource	Creative practical activities
	Guess what the object is?
Digital camera close-up photographs of various objects, e.g. pineapple	Observational drawings of small parts of the looking for detail. Learners take close-up photographs and challenge others to identify them.
Eyes	Looking at each other's eyes. Noticing the different colours of eyes. Recording their friends' eyes using wool stuck on card. Covering eyes and observe change in pupils.

(Continued)

Resource	Creative practical activities
Baby teeth Toothbrush Toothpaste	Looking at different shapes of teeth and their function. Mixing toothpastes with water and observing how much foam occurs and whether all the toothpaste dissolves.
Looking at different animal bones	What animal did it come from? How do you know? What ways are they the same? What are the differences? Which bone might have belonged to a mouse and which an elephant? Close observation using digital microscope.
Woolly jumper	Close observation of wool. Looking at where the wool comes from and how it is treated to become the jumper. Wool under the digital microscope.
Archimedes thermometer	Watching the liquid filled bulbs rise and fall with temperature. Exploring how other water filled things float and sink. Cartesian divers.
Sponges	Observation, what is it made from? Man-made and natural sponges. How much water does it absorb? Will it float or sink? How many holes are there and is there a pattern between holes and sinking/water absorbency?
Ice cube	How can you keep an ice cube in the classroom for the longest time? What could be designed? Create an ice-cube holder.
Sand and yoghurt pots in a tray or sand tray	What proportion of sand and water do you need to make a good sandcastle?
Poppy seed heads	Seed dispersal. Thinking about what it might look like inside. What colour and size might the seeds be?
Seed packets: a variety of types need to be observed and discussed	Look at the picture of the plants on the seed packet. How big do learners think the seed will be and why do they think this? What colour do they think they will be? Young learners often think that tall plants will have big seeds and will be the same colour as the resulting plant. Opening the seed-packet is often very exciting for very young learners and can lead to questions to test whether the

(Continued)

Table 1.1   (Continued)

Resource	Creative practical activities
	biggest seed produces the biggest plant. This can lead immediately to further investigation to extend learners' experience of seeds and plants beyond cress. (Δ Ensure seeds are not treated with pesticides.)
Hole-punch	How does it work? What does the spring do? Link to forces. Looking at other springs, e.g. pogo sticks. Helps learners make connections.
Deflated balloon, ice balloon, water balloon, air balloon	Initial observation of the 4 balloons will lead to noticing differences and similarities between them. Learners can be asked to describe each of the balloons and the vocabulary used noted. Younger learners can have their observations scribed for them. What learners notice about the balloons could lead to many questions. Learners can be asked to raise questions. Questions raised can then be 'scanned' by the teacher for productive questions and these can lead to specific activities, e.g. What happened when they are put in water? Will each balloon bounce? How high will it bounce? How high will it bounce on different surfaces? What is the weight of the balloons? Here younger learners can compare weights, older learners can use instruments to measure.
Bubbles	Bubbles provide an excellent starting point for many observations. Vocabulary can be noted, observations can be shared and, if necessary, revisited. Different sizes and shapes of wands can be used to find out whether the shape of the wand affects the shape of the bubbles.
Tea bags	Looking at the similarities and differences between tea bags. Close examination of different bags under a hand lens and digital microscope to find out the size of the holes. Weighing the tea in different bags. Looking at the shape of the tea leaves under a digital microscope. Making tea at not more than 60 degrees Celsius. Looking at the colour of

(Continued)

Table 1.1 (Continued)

Resource	Creative practical activities
	different teas. Which tea bag makes the strongest tea in five minutes? What happens when you soak fabrics in the tea?
Soap	Which soap washes paint off quickest? Warm and cold water can also be tested. How long before feet go wrinkly? Placing feet in warm water and seeing how long before they wrinkle. Drawing feet after. How much lather does a bar make? Testing different types of soap, turning the bar in hands once and then rubbing them together and comparing amounts of lather.

Summary

This chapter has considered a number of important points related to science, the nature of science and the approach of science in the primary curriculum. It has shown that science knowledge and understanding has to be provided for alongside the development of procedural understanding and process skills; that for the future well-being of the individual and society learners' attitudes towards and in science must not be ignored.

There is a need to move away from the view that promotes science as a stuffy subject full of facts to be learned. This view needs to be replaced with an approach to teaching that envisions science and the teaching of science as a creative activity. If this is to be successful, then teachers need to give full consideration to learners' ideas and to utilise these to further learners' understanding of science in everyday life. The challenge for today's primary teacher is to break from the traditional mould and to teach science in a creative way making it more relevant to the future generation of 'could be' scientists.

Further Reading

Hamblin, A.H. Foster, J.R. (2000) Ancient Animal footprints and Traces in the Grandstaircase-Escalante National monument, South Central Utah. *Utah Geological Association Publication 28* can be downloaded from www.utahgeology.org/pub28_pdf_rules/Hamblin.pdf.

Harlen, W. (2006) 'The goals of science education', in *Teaching Learning and Assessing Science 5–12*. London: Sage.

Osborne, J.F., Duschl, R. et al. (2002) *Breaking the Mould: Teaching Science for Public Understanding.* London: Nuffield Foundation.

Osborne, J. F., Ratcliffe, M., Collins, S., Millar, R. and Duschl, R. (2003) 'What "ideas-about-science" should be taught in school science?' A Delphi Study of the 'Expert' Community, *Journal of Research in Science Teaching*, 40(7): 692–720.

2

The Skills Learners Need to Learn Science – Process Skills

Hellen Ward and Judith Roden

Introduction

This chapter will explore the process skills and their role in developing learners' knowledge and understanding of science. It will identify and consider the importance of developing these skills. Although termed the process skills, the skills needed to learn science, in everyday teaching and learning in schools are also known as the basic skills. These basic skills, while sometimes implicit rather than explicit, are embedded into Sc1, Scientific Enquiry: the backbone of the National Curriculum. The main aim of this chapter is to look at ways in which teachers can structure the experiences they provide to learners to develop these skills within the science topic or unit of work.

Developing Learners' Process Skills

Initially, learners' process skills are limited and unsystematic, characterised by trial and error exploration. It is part of the teacher's role to help to develop these so that as they mature, learners approach the exploration of the world in a more systematic, organised and meaningful way. Unconsciously, young learners make use of simple individual process skills all the time during their exploration of the world but, as they get older, individual skills become more important in their formal education. The simpler skills involve observing, classifying, questioning and hypothesising, but these are fundamental to the development of more advanced skills such as planning, predicting and data interpretation.

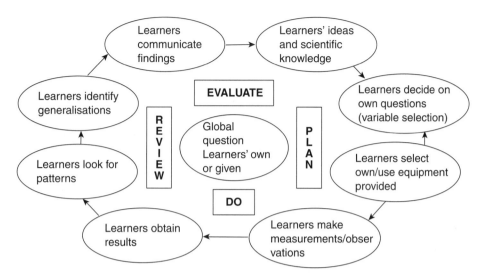

Figure 2.1   Process skills

As learners move through school, teachers need to identify the individual process skills that together make up procedural understanding e.g. observation or the ability to raise questions and plan to provide the opportunities for learners to practise these individually within activities where the learning intention is related explicitly to the chosen process skill. This will not only allow improved application of individual skills, but, over time, more sophisticated use of the whole process. The result being that the overall quality of learners' engagement in scientific enquiry is raised. This implies that teachers need to identify individual process skills at the planning stage and to focus learning objectives on them. Success here relies on careful planning, focusing on process skill intentions alongside those related to knowledge and understanding.

Within scientific enquiry learners use a number of process skills separately and together depending on the activity presented to them. Observation is a basic skill that links many of the other identified processes, but leads into and enhances the quality of other process skills, for example, questions often arise out of small details noticed by observation and also the quality of data collected in an investigation. Questions raised either by the teacher or learners themselves can be used as a starting point for investigations of all kinds. Process skills are important, but their use depends on the learners' previous experience of using them and on their previous knowledge and understanding of the topic under study:

Prediction is a well practised skill involved in scientific enquiry. It depends on previous experience of the focus of study. When a prediction is linked with an explanation, no matter how simple, this is called a hypothesis. Hypotheses can be tested. Planning, obtaining and presenting evidence, considering and evaluating are all elements of scientific enquiry. Equipment selection is also important here. Learners should be encouraged to make use of higher-level skills at an appropriate level for themselves. Obtaining and presenting evidence includes learners in making measurements using both standard and non-standard units, using equipment with varying degrees of precision. Importantly, learners also need to think about the potential hazards and risks within their planned investigation and consider safe working related to themselves and to others.

Once data is collected, learners need to look for patterns and trends in order to draw their own conclusions in doing so. Explaining what they have found out enables them to make sense of their findings and allows them to use their increasing scientific vocabulary to optimise overall learning.

Questioning and Question-Raising

It is widely accepted that learners bring previous knowledge to a new situation and this forms the basis upon which to extend their understanding. In order to extend their knowledge, learners should be encouraged to ask questions about the world around them. Being asked to raise questions and to find their own answers enables learners to relate new ideas to a previous experience and to draw upon their current knowledge and understanding. Although they find this challenging, learners will, and do with encouragement, raise their own appropriate questions that can be investigated. Questioning, alongside observation and enquiry, is a key aspect of developing learners' understanding of the world. Learners need to understand the difference between the questions they ask that can be investigated, those that will be answered using other approaches and those that do not have an answer. Clearly, then, it is important to encourage learners' questions and there are a variety of ways to do this.

The use of a 'question box' in the classroom helps involve the learners in the learning process. Learners post their questions about the unit of work under study and these questions are then selected by the teacher and focused upon on a weekly basis. This helps to show that the learners' questions are important and valued, and links them effectively into classroom work. It is also a good idea to have a 'problem' corner or a 'question of the week' for learners to pursue in their free time. Displays can include enquiry questions, and a question board is another strategy that encourages the involvement of learners. The questions are shared in a visual way and learners can then find the answers and add these to the wall display (Figure 2.2). The answers can come from work in lessons as well as self-study or homework activities.

The KWHL grid (K = What I know; W = What I want to know; H = How I will find out; L = What I have learned) also facilitates the raising of learners' questions at the start of a unit of work. The items in the 'Know' column can be used to focus upon areas of misconception and the questions raised can encourage learners' interest in lessons. Although not all of the questions will be asked in a form that can be investigated practically, many can be used as a starting point for appropriate practical work and others will be answered by using secondary sources.

While pre-school learners seem continually to ask questions, some older learners seem to have lost this ability. This might be because traditional teaching has not required learners to ask questions or, more often, learners are not

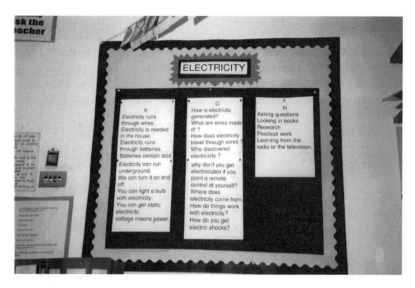

Figure 2.2   Displaying learners' questions and the answers found

encouraged to ask questions because teachers have been afraid of not knowing the answers. In recent years learners' questions have been somewhat irrelevant, with the trend towards the widespread use of inflexible schemes of work that provide little opportunity for work to be tailored to meet the needs of individuals. Worryingly, a HMI report (2004) suggests that although teachers elicit learners' original ideas, little action is taken to alter the work planned to tailor the work to the identified learning needs elicited by this process. With an introduction to a more creative curriculum, a more flexible approach is now more possible than before.

Enabling learners to define their own questions is an important feature of investigative work. This should take place initially in basic skills lessons, as learners need to be taught how to ask investigative questions. It would be ideal if learners could, following this starting point, go on to try out their ideas. However, time for science in the primary curriculum has become squeezed in recent years and therefore time to follow through all starting points to a complete investigation would not, in itself, enable the basic skill of questioning to be developed.

Global Questions

Teachers can help to scaffold learners' learning in investigative work by providing a 'global question' as a starting point. This enables the learners to begin to identify variables, offering a way whereby learners can generate appropriate questions within an investigative framework.

Using the global question 'How can we keep a drink hot for the longest time?' provides the opportunity to identify many variables. However, in a lesson where the focus is upon the skill of question-raising, it is important for the teacher to select the variables to be used, for example, selecting the factor to change (independent variables) as 'the type of liquid' and the factor to measure (the dependent variable) as 'temperature over time'. From this starting point learners can then identify specific questions and this process should be supported by modelling and shared writing. The questions that result could be 'What happens to the temperature of different liquids over time?' or 'What happens to the temperature of liquids over time?' or even 'Which liquid will cool the quickest?' Discussion, alteration and refinement of these questions can then occur, further developing the learners' skills in question-raising.

Modelling allows learners to develop their skills further than if they were unaided, however, the degree of support should be reduced over time. Learners should be provided with opportunities to practise their newly developed skills, i.e. given the opportunity to generate new questions using the same global question but with different variables. For example, if, instead of the type of liquid, the independent variable could be changed to 'the type of materials the cup is made from', different questions will be formulated, such as 'Which material will keep a drink hotter for longer?' or 'Which material is the most effective at keeping a drink hot?' or 'What happens to the temperature of the liquid in different types of cup?' Some learners' questions will be more refined than others and discussion of this should be a teaching point so that gradually they begin to identify better questions. Eventually learners will ask better questions and go on to identify global questions for themselves.

Variable Identification and Selection

Variables are also called 'factors'. Those that can be changed are termed the independent variables, while those that can be observed and/or measured are called the dependent variables.

At the beginning it is useful to ask learners to identify all the variables for an investigation. Using a global question is a good starting point. For example using the global question 'How can we keep an ice cube from melting?', with some prompting from the teacher, learners should be able to identify what could be changed in order to keep the ice cube from melting. In this example, the independent variables include the type of material, the amount of material, the size of the ice cube and the position of the ice cube. When given the opportunity, learners do not usually find identifying variables difficult; in fact, they often enjoy the challenge.

Identifying the dependent variables is more problematic. These are the outcomes of the test, the temperature drop of the liquid or the time taken for the ice cube to melt. Some learners will identify with the term 'measurement' and will think of measuring the ice. However, the amount of ice is one of the variables that can be changed and just measuring the amount of ice will not lead to data that will answer their question. Highlighting the different variables for changing and measuring using different-coloured 'Post-it' notes, one colour for those variables that can be changed and another colour for those that can be measured, helps the learners to identify and recognise these different features (Figure 2.3).

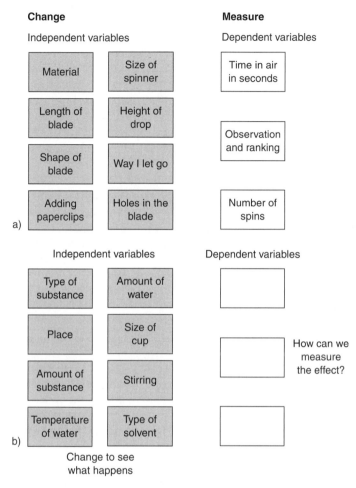

Figure 2.3 Post-it notes and skills lessons for variable and question-raising skills lessons. In (a) What is the question? or (b) what could the dependent variables be?

Predicting

Prediction is commonly practised in most primary classrooms. In fact, this could be seen as one of the key outcomes of the National Curriculum's impact on practice at Key Stages 1 and 2. Prediction making, currently, is probably one of the few science skills focused upon in many infant and junior classrooms. Many lessons start with the question 'What do you think will happen?' before any equipment is used or any activity is undertaken. While prediction is an important skill, perhaps this emphasis or overemphasis should be evaluated.

With very young learners, asking for a prediction will often result in the response 'I don't know'. Using the ubiquitous 'cars down ramps' scenario, where learners are asked which car will travel the furthest after being let go at the top of a ramp, often results in learners selecting a car of a particular colour because it is their favourite. This is the 'I like blue, because blue is the best' response. Learners, at this stage, do not have a well-defined or developed understanding of why things happen and yet they are frequently asked to make a prediction. The result of this emphasis is twofold. First, learners are asked to make a prediction when their knowledge and understanding of the aspect are limited and, secondly, teachers pre-judge an outcome. When carrying out work with the cars, the learners either find that their ideas are wrong, so they 'cheat' to ensure their prediction becomes correct, or they change their prediction to match the findings, understanding only that they were wrong. Sadly, the learners unconsciously receive the inappropriate message that making a prediction is an element of science that 'proves' that science has the right answer and that perhaps their role is to find it.

Teachers often also expect that the outcomes of activities will 'prove' fact. It is really important that learners are allowed to carry out their own investigation, collect and interpret their own data and then consider what their data tells them, i.e. draw their own conclusions based on consideration of the collected evidence. It is tempting for teachers, anxious for their learners to get the 'right answer', to suggest that some data are disregarded.

Case Study 2.1

One group of Year 6 learners, working on a topic of mini-beasts, carried out a simple practical task to find out where woodlice like to live. The learners were asked to test different materials and to set up a survey. They were given a shoebox with a lid and a range of materials with which to line sections of the box to find out if the woodlice had preferences. The learners carried out their observational activities and recorded the time the woodlice spent in the different places by time sampling and tallying the numbers of individuals in each location. The results of all the groups were fed back to the teacher at the end of 30 minutes.

The result was that all but one of the groups demonstrated that the woodlice preferred the damp area. However, one group found that their woodlice spent more time in the straw. Although their findings did not concur with other groups', their results were consistent with the data collected by their observations. These unexpected results neither tallied with their own prediction, nor with that of their class teacher. Unfortunately, the teacher stated that their results were wrong and that they should not write their findings as their conclusion. Worryingly, they were required to write the conclusions obtained by the rest of the class.

Pre-judging an outcome is problematic because it promotes the idea that there is one answer and that the learners' role is to hunt it out! This is not helpful to learner learning and does not reflect the way in which scientists work. Professor Lewis Wolpert, one of the Acclaim scientists (www.acclaimscientists.org.uk), when asked what would he do if his experiment did not work, stated 'Try to understand why'. It is important here to note that science develops through things that do not work as much as through those that do and that this is true also of how learners' understanding of science develops.

It is clear from Attainment Target 1 Level Descriptors of the National Curriculum (DfES, 1999) that making a prediction first appears at Level 4. This is the expectation for an average Year 6 learner. At Level 2 the expectation is that learners should be asked about their ideas after they have finished their work. Yet, in common practice, even young learners are continually asked to give a reason for why things might happen in advance of them happening. Even adults, when asked to give a prediction if they have no previous experience or knowledge to use, are actually put off. In the same way, asking young learners to make a prediction when they have little prior evidence to apply to the situation can be equally off-putting and threatening. Therefore teachers should refrain from formally requesting a prediction in every activity. This view does not, however, preclude the teacher from taking notice if learners spontaneously provide suggestions about what they think might happen. This could be recorded on the learners' work and reflected upon with them, at a later time. In fact, this would indicate good practice, not least in terms of differentiation.

Equipment Selection and Use

In the early years of primary education, learners are often expected to use equipment provided for them by their teacher and only later are they required to select their own. However, it is difficult for learners to choose appropriate instruments to use if they have had limited experience of using relevant resources. Therefore, learners need to be shown particular pieces of equipment and need to be taught explicitly how to use them. While it is common practice in mathematics for time to be spent on teaching learners how to use equipment using a range of approaches, in science, equipment is often introduced as part of an activity. Instead, scientific equipment should be introduced to the learners and should be the focus of the learning intention within an illustrative activity. This then not only allows learners to make an informed choice about which equipment to use in an activity, but will enable them to use the equipment correctly and make more accurate measurements.

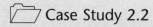 Case Study 2.2

Using a Newton meter is a prime example of a resource that is often not introduced before it is used. When first introduced, many learners are not often aware of forces in everyday life, let alone aware of how they may be measured. Before the Newton meter or spring balance is introduced to learners they need to have had opportunities to push objects with springs to see the effects of this on the spring. Following this they should go on

(Continued)

(Continued)

to pull and contract springs as part of simple work on forces. (Springs are not expensive pieces of equipment and bags of 500 springs suitable for this purpose can be bought very cheaply.) Learners should then be introduced to a range of Newton meters and asked to find similarities and differences between them (10N and 20N, or 10N and 5N). The teachers should then allow the learners to explore using the Newton meters. Initially teachers should model how to do this, as less equipment is broken when learners are taught how to hold the meters correctly. The correct way to hold the Newton meter is to hold it at the top with one hand and to place a little finger of the other hand in the hook at the bottom. Learners need to pull down on the hook gently, using only the little finger. Then, the adult should ask questions to focus the learners' attention. 'What happens to the spring when you pull down gently?' 'What happens to the spring when you stop pulling and allow the spring to return?' Changing over to different types of Newton meters enables learners to obtain information in order to make generalisations. The bigger and thicker the spring, the harder it is to pull. Playing a guessing game in pairs helps learners to gain an understanding of this measurement of force. While one learner places their little finger on the hook of the Newton meter and closes their eyes, the other learner holds the top and asks the first learner to pull a force of a set number of Newtons, e.g. 4N. When the learner who is pulling thinks he or she has pulled the requested amount of force, the pupil opens their eyes and check the scale. With learners changing over roles and using different force meters they not only become very accurate in estimation and scale reading, but also gain a clearer idea of what a Newton feels like.

It is crucial that, before learners are asked to make and record measurements, they have been introduced to the relevant equipment in this way, otherwise their results will not be accurate, and therefore not reliable, and the learners will not be able to explain their findings.

Fair-Testing

Learners need some guidance when they are identifying the independent and the dependent variables. Although often identified as one of the process skills, fair-testing is actually a procedure of science. This procedure provides a platform to enable learners to carry out the work in a scientific way, called the fair test. Whilst fair-testing is only one aspect of the scientific method, it is the aspect focused upon extensively in the primary science curriculum. This has led to many learners and teachers seeing the 'fair test' as the only method of practical science and, often, most science activities are carried out using the fair-test model whether this is appropriate or not. The method is confusing for young learners because of the term 'fair', which to them means not to cheat or everyone 'having a turn'.

Scientifically, a fair test is one where only one variable is changed and all the rest remain constant. It is the inability to keep all the factors constant that makes this method ineffective for some investigations. Plants, humans and other animals are living things with genetic differences. These differences can play havoc with the result unless large enough samples are used. These other factors, the hidden ones, also affect results. A good example of a hidden factor can be demonstrated using the simple plants experiment.

 ## Case Study 2.3

> In a typical lesson on plants the factors that affect growth are selected. The teacher and learners talk about what to test, and decide upon altering the amount of light, keeping the amount of water, soil, type of plant, etc. the same. The outcome is to be measured by comparing the height or colour of the leaves. One plant is placed on the windowsill, one in a cupboard and another under a table, and a fair test is started. However, the plant on the windowsill does not grow as expected. This plant experiences the greatest range of temperatures, as it is in the hottest place in the day and the coldest place at night, sometimes by as much as 20°C. This temperature change is a hidden factor which can cause the plant, and the teacher, stress. Another hidden factor is the genetic make-up of the plant. Both will impact upon the results and make it difficult to 'prove' the point being illustrated. A survey using more plants and obtaining a greater range of information would have been scientifically more accurate or 'fair'.

Extending the types of investigations that the learners are exposed to is essential. Going back to watching and recording change over time, surveying, problem solving and observations are vital. By planting a number of bean plants at the rate of one a day for two weeks, and monitoring their growth, the practical skills developed as a result are far greater than those which would have been obtained from watching one seed germinate. This is not an investigation but an observational task – a valid science activity – and will provide the learners with opportunities to learn about science and then use these skills to carry out their own investigations. However, in order for this to take place, more value and status must be given to non-fair test activities and a greater understanding of methods of science is needed. In the 1800s, about 300 stones fell from the sky near a village in France called Laigle. Before the stones landed there were bright lights in the sky and the stones made craters in the ground. Using data collected from observations, scientists decided that the rocks had come from space. This deduction had no fair test element or planning attached to it, however, it was still effective science. The scientists obviously did not plan this event, but the method of gaining understanding about the world was still a valid one. Observations can be planned, and an immense amount of planning and testing occurred prior to the invention of the first microscope. Valuing other aspects of science, in addition to the fair test, is vital if progress is to be made in developing creative-thinking individuals for the future. This would be more common if an ideas and evidence approach was used.

Checking Observation and Data

Once observations and measurements have been made it is important that learners critique these. Taking more than one reading in a practical investigation is expected from the end of Key Stage 1, although the expectation is that 7-year-olds will add the totals or take the middle number. At this stage, looking at the readings and checking for odd results must be simply taught. Checking readings allows the reliability of the readings to be gauged. Learners can be taught to identify unusual results and to repeat these. This skill should be taught in basic skills lessons and then should be practised during complete investigations.

Using a Range of Recording Strategies

Currently, creativity in science is being stifled by the use of a limited number of methodologies and outdated recording strategies. Learners are often expected to record using the traditional method, the 'apparatus, result and conclusion' approach, for every piece of work. While practice in literacy has developed over the last decade with the introduction of skill-based lessons, this has not happened in science teaching. There is no primary science strategy to guide teachers towards alternative recording methods and for many teachers their only experience of science has been gained from their own secondary-school education. Rather than learners being required to record what they have done and their findings in a more imaginative way, an outdated method of recording is disadvantaging both the less literate and more literate alike. The method of recording adopted is often as a result of requiring evidence of work completed to be in the learners' books. Worse still, the work is often written on the board by the teacher for learners to copy. While the modelling and support that are sometimes provided in this shared writing element are recommended, the copying of the shared text by all learners is as unacceptable in science as it would be in literacy, because it is just handwriting practice.

This practice does little to fire the imagination of young impressionable learners as their attitudes towards science are being formed. An HMI report suggested that many learners could not even read the work that they had written in their books. Instead, learners should be encouraged to use pictures, drawings and diagrams as well as cartoon strips, poems and posters to record their work in science (see, for example, Figure 2.4).

To have the greatest impact, recording should occur throughout the lesson, not just at the end. Learners need to be introduced to the different ways of recording in the same way as they need to be introduced to resources. Teachers need to select a different method of recording to model, and where possible this should be the focus of the learning intention. This then enables a range of recording opportunities to be provided throughout the year so that at a later stage, when learners are asked to choose their own, most appropriate, method, they have a repertoire from which to select.

The use of word banks and individual learner science dictionaries promotes learner independence. Recording in science also requires mathematical skills of drawing tables and graphs. Modelling and breaking these activities down into small steps helps learners to develop their recording skills.

Identifying Patterns, Trends in Data and Data Interpretation

Learners need to be taught how to present data, for example, drawing diagrams and graphs, as well as having the opportunity to interpret these. Interpreting data relies heavily on seeing patterns or relationships between things that can be observed. This skill is closely linked with the skill of evaluating. Specific lessons need to be planned across the key stage where time is devoted to this skill, enabling learners to find the patterns and draw inferences for themselves. An important part of pattern-seeking is being able to describe what is seen. Learners therefore need the support of the teacher to develop the appropriate vocabulary and to know what to identify. Pattern-seeking is about describing what is seen rather than explaining why it happens. Providing graphs and asking questions related to these enables learners to learn how to interpret the graphs. This is initially difficult for many learners as graphing skills usually focus upon the drawing of the minutiae rather than the broad patterns within.

Identifying the patterns and trends would rarely take up a complete science lesson, so after identifying the patterns and trends the learners can then try out one of the tasks. As learners often have difficulties in interpreting patterns and trends, starting a lesson in this way is helpful. Frequently, insufficient time is devoted to this aspect of learning in science as these tasks are often left to the end of an illustrative or investigative activity. Consequently, for many learners, their ability to identify patterns, to see trends in data and to interpret what their data tell them is often underdeveloped. They are not being provided with sufficient opportunity to develop the higher-order skills in science, because carrying out the activity and recording the result are viewed as more important.

Drawing Graphs

Drawing graphs is hard! The process of graph-drawing requires spatial awareness and teachers need to provide learners with support for graph-making. A good

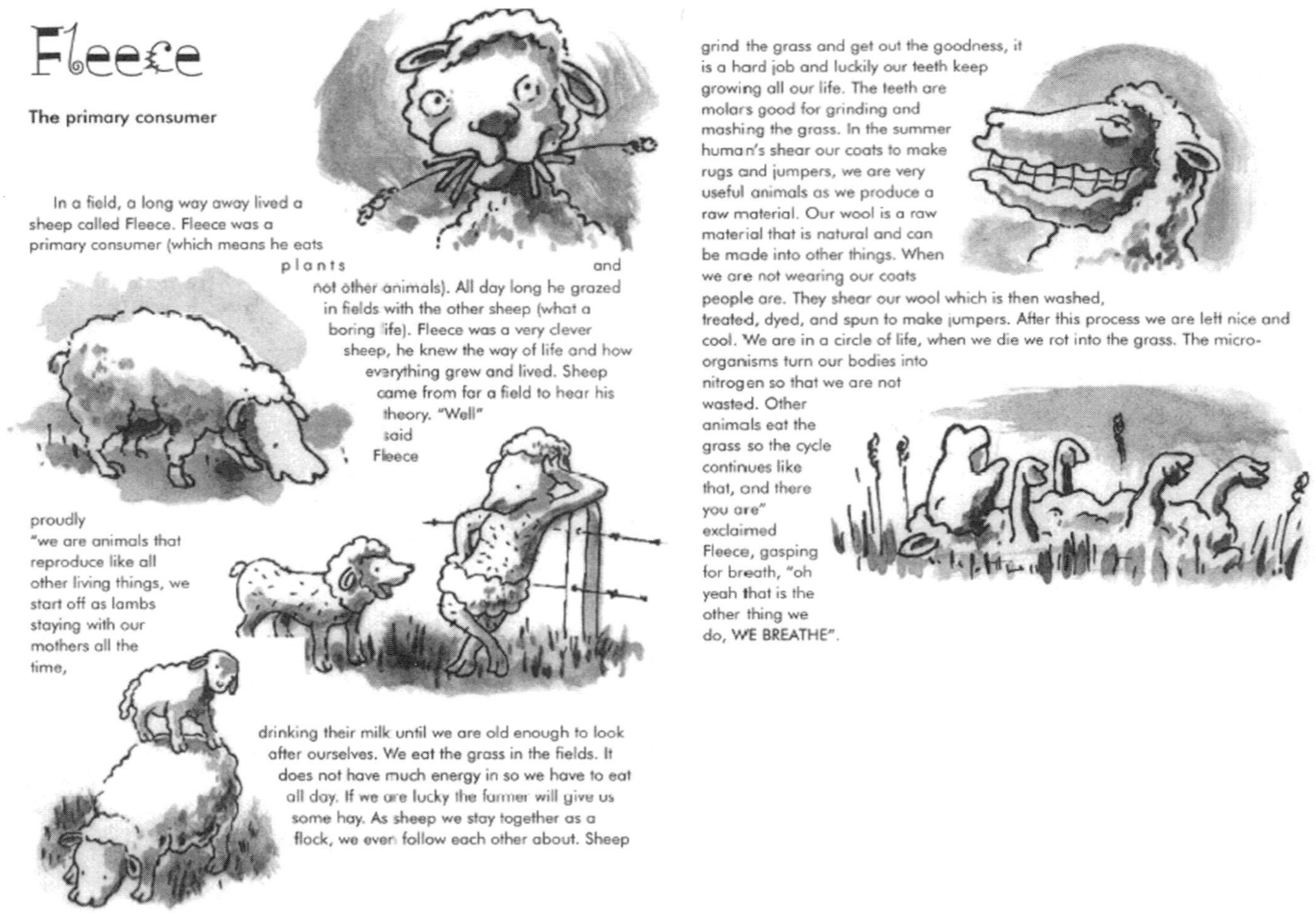

Fleece

The primary consumer

In a field, a long way away lived a sheep called Fleece. Fleece was a primary consumer (which means he eats plants and not other animals). All day long he grazed in fields with the other sheep (what a boring life). Fleece was a very clever sheep, he knew the way of life and how everything grew and lived. Sheep came from far a field to hear his theory. "Well" said Fleece proudly "we are animals that reproduce like all other living things, we start off as lambs staying with our mothers all the time, drinking their milk until we are old enough to look after ourselves. We eat the grass in the fields. It does not have much energy in so we have to eat all day. If we are lucky the farmer will give us some hay. As sheep we stay together as a flock, we even follow each other about. Sheep grind the grass and get out the goodness, it is a hard job and luckily our teeth keep growing all our life. The teeth are molars good for grinding and mashing the grass. In the summer human's shear our coats to make rugs and jumpers, we are very useful animals as we produce a raw material. Our wool is a raw material that is natural and can be made into other things. When we are not wearing our coats people are. They shear our wool which is then washed, treated, dyed, and spun to make jumpers. After this process we are left nice and cool. We are in a circle of life, when we die we rot into the grass. The micro-organisms turn our bodies into nitrogen so that we are not wasted. Other animals eat the grass so the cycle continues like that, and there you are" exclaimed Fleece, gasping for breath, "oh yeah that is the other thing we do, WE BREATHE".

Figure 2.4 Fleece is a story by a Year 6 child.

introduction is to start with examples of graphs that have mistakes on them, as asking learners to 'spot the deliberate mistakes' helps them to identify what features a graph should contain. Teaching learners graph-drawing skills and allowing opportunities to practise these skills does work. Learners can become very good at drawing graphs, and this can be related directly to detailed teaching. When interpreting data is the learning intention, rather than the drawing of a graph itself, the labour and time involved in drawing a graph can be minimised by use of a computer program.

Conclusions

Drawing conclusions makes learners aware of what they have discovered and why it is relevant, but few learners find this easy. Concluding is a crucial, basic skill that is made easier if learners have developed enough appropriate scientific vocabulary. Providing opportunities for learners to evaluate conclusions written by others, especially if this is undertaken as an aspect of peer assessment, supports this process and helps learners to identify what are the features of good explanations and how they differ from descriptions. Providing skills lessons that focus upon a set of prewritten conclusions with modelling and scaffolding by the teacher is vital. Learners should not write down the statements or conclusions that have been modelled with them, but should always try to improve or alter the ones that have been discussed. This process also supports scientific understanding and the content of the statements can be altered in order to target the skill of drawing appropriate conclusions based on evidence.

Evaluation

Evaluation is an important process skill following an investigation. The evaluation of the way in which an activity proceeded is required, as is questioning the reliability of the data collected. Learners need to review, critically, the methods used in order to make suggestions for future work. They also need to discuss what they have done and why, and to think about how else they might have completed the task or recorded the information. This allows learners to actively evaluate their own and others' learning. Providing a structure for this to happen, such as a series of questions, scaffolds the process. Where learners are not supported in this process they often evaluate the work in a non-scientific way, for example, in one case a group of 10-year-olds were asked to evaluate the work: 'It would have been better if Kirsty had not been sick in the bucket' was the response. A group of infants, who were not used to investigating or evaluating their work, suggested 'It was fun, do not change it at all'! However, the question needs to be asked if children are to become more skilled in their ability to evaluate.

Summary

The importance of the process skills that are needed in order to undertake scientific enquiry has been highlighted throughout this chapter. The chapter has shown the need for teachers to plan directly for the development of individual science process skills and to include activities in science that will enable learners to develop these progressively and systematically throughout their time in school, thus developing procedural understanding. The chapters that follow will consider these issues in more depth; for example, the next chapter will focus more specifically on the skill of observation. Chapter 5 will expand on these skills and show how they are linked in investigating an idea.

Further Reading

Alfredo, T., Natale, N. and Lombardi, A. (2006) 'Scientists at play: teaching science process skills', *Science in School*, 1: 37–40. www.scienceinschool.org.uk

Harlen, W. and Qualter, A. (2004) 'Ways of helping the development of process skills', in *The Teaching of Science in Primary Schools*. London: David Fulton.

Milne, I. (2007) 'Children's Science', *Primary Science Review*, 100.

3

Observation, Measurement and Classification

Judith Roden

Introduction

This chapter will explore why it is important for learners to be regularly provided with activities to develop their observation, measurement and classification skills, and also to provide suggestions for a range of activities that will help teachers to plan worthwhile activities for systematic study. Additionally, it will provide an explanation of how these can contribute to learners' learning in science.

Developing the Skills of Observation, Measurement and Classification

Observation, measurement and classification are fundamental aspects of scientific enquiry at all key stages of the primary school. In order to develop learners' knowledge and understanding of the world at the Foundation Stage, practitioners should give particular attention to activities based on first-hand exploration. Building on this experience, it is important that older learners collect evidence by making observations and measurements when trying to answer a question, and later that they test ideas, including those of their own, using evidence from observation and measurement.

One point of note here is that the development of the process skills of observation, measurement and classification as a simple type of investigation that relies on theses should not be taught separately, but should be set in the context of other specific scientific topics within a scheme of work. This means that teachers should focus learning intentions specifically on observation, measurement and classification, and they should regularly provide specific tasks that require learners to make observations and measurements in relation to things in the living world, materials and their properties and physical processes, using these as a basis for classification.

It is crucial that learners are provided with opportunities to observe, measure and classify, noticing the finer detail of things, and that this should be included in schemes of work across the whole of the 3–11-year age range. This not only helps to interrelate scientific enquiry into the other aspects of science, but also should enable learners to build up an understanding of things systematically across the various aspects of science. For example, when looking at aspects of life in the living world, learners could observe things from the natural living world, such as small creatures, leaves or flowers, etc. By doing so, learners will also develop their understanding of, for example, the diversity of living things, the parts of a flower or parts of a leaf. Observation and drawing of a number of different kinds of pine cones, or rocks, or shells, will reveal the differences there are between things which are similar. In the same way, in relation to materials and their properties, learners could look closely at a variety of fabrics, or paper, or wood, which could lead to simple investigations to find out, for example, which fabric absorbs the most water, or which is the best wrapping paper with which to wrap up Christmas parcels, or which is the best paper for writing on. When the focus of study is on physical processes, learners might be encouraged to note the finer parts of unconnected small light bulbs. Here, noting similarities and differences between bulbs of different voltages may well lead directly to questions about the size of filaments and simple investigations to find out what happens when the different bulbs are connected, one by one, into the same simple electrical circuits.

Observational drawings provide excellent opportunities for learners to record their observations and measurements. Here, teacher questions should focus on learners looking for detail and patterns, etc. Some might argue that observational drawing is more of an art than a science activity; however, in science it is different because the learning intentions are different. The learning intention in science is not about the quality of the drawing, although accuracy in drawing might be encouraged, but more about recording observed features, noticing detail and patterns, and identifying similarities and differences.

The use of frames or 'peepholes' can focus learners' observations on a small area to view specific details rather than on gross external features. Use of peepholes provides a less threatening situation than asking learners to draw a whole object, as only one small part has to be focused on. It is important to realise that it is legitimate, and important, to have process skills learning intentions in addition to those relating to knowledge and understanding, or sometimes exclusively. These should be indicated explicitly in long- , medium- and short-term plans as well as in lesson plans. It is important to remember that here the focus is on developing the process skills.

Progression in what is expected from learners is important in terms of observation, measurement and classification as they progress through the early and primary years. Consequently, while activities provided for learners may be similar in nature at the different levels, teachers need to place different expectations on different individuals and groups of learners to ensure challenge and linear progression in learning.

Why Learners should be Taught to Observe

Clearly, observation is important: it is a fundamental aspect of the learning process and, although the skill is taken much for granted in everyday life, it is crucial for making sense of the world from an early age. Without this first-hand experience, learners may not question what is observed in their world. Observation provides the opportunity for learners to explore the nature of objects and the relationship between objects. Observation and, more importantly, as they get older, critical observation promotes scientific thinking and contributes to learners' understanding of science. Furthermore, initial observations can lead to the formulation of questions, hypotheses, predictions and conclusions.

Observation is also one of the most important process skills for developing knowledge of the natural and physical world. Here observation provides a good starting point for further exploration and investigation. It is widely accepted that learners and adults learn about the world by using all their senses – touch, sight, smell, taste and hearing – and so learners should regularly, when appropriate and with care, be asked to undertake activities specifically planned to develop the skill. Observation is therefore an important process skill, because it develops the ability to use all the senses appropriately and safely, which enables learners to find patterns and develops the ability to sort and classify.

The role of the teacher in helping learners to observe is crucial here, as what teachers ask learners to look for can have a significant effect on what is observed. Additionally, what learners see is influenced by what they already know. Therefore, focused observation not only helps learners to identify differences and similarities between objects or situations, but also helps them to see previously unnoticed patterns and to provide questions to be investigated further.

It is generally recognised that learners find it more difficult to notice similarities because differences are often more obvious. Learners also need to be encouraged to look for patterns and sequences in a series of observations especially in illustrative activities and investigations.

Ultimately, systematic observation, especially when collecting data, for example, when measuring the temperature of water as it cools, results in accurate observations.

Developing the skill of observation is important not only for the individual, but also for the wider development of scientific knowledge and understanding within the larger scientific community. In the past, great leaps in the development of scientific ideas have come about from an initial starting point where noticing a small, possibly unusual, observation has led to a search for a new explanation to explain the observations or inconsistencies. This helps to explain how revolutions in scientific thinking have come about: for example, Newton's observation of the apple falling from a tree, Archimedes' observations of water levels or Priestley's exploration of what happens when something burns.

Figure 3.1   Close-up photograph of broccoli

What Sort of Activities can Help Learners to Develop their Observation Skills?

There are many basic observation activities that can be used across the age range. For example, at the earliest stages of education, observation enables learners to gain information about a wide variety of different everyday objects. Learners should regularly be asked to describe, for example, a leaf, an apple, a book or a table fork, thus enabling them to see similarities and differences between things that are very different. Building on this foundation, older learners can be asked to describe objects that are very similar, such as a number of different leaves, pine cones, seashells, rocks, etc. This leads to the recognition of characteristics by which scientists group things together. Older learners need to be challenged to observe finer detail. This can be made more challenging by asking more able and older learners for measurements to be included in the description.

A good activity for making learners look more closely at objects makes use of a digital camera. Providing learners with close-up photographs of an object and then asking them to identify the object from the picture is a good way to encourage fine observation. If learners cannot identify the object immediately they can be challenged to 'go find the object'. This is a fun way to improve finer observational skills and learners enjoy the experience. Younger learners can be provided with photographs that may well seem obvious to older learners and adults, for example see Figure 3.1.

Learners can be given a range of close-up photographs and the real objects can be placed around the room. Learners are challenged to match the photo

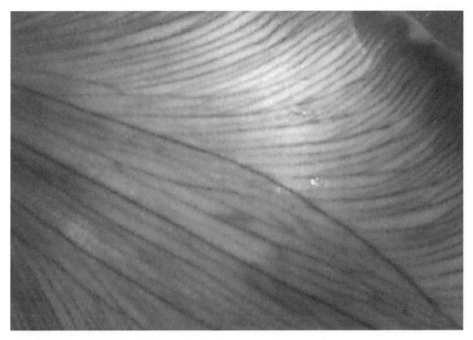

Figure 3.2 Close-up photograph of a flower petal

with the real object and asked to identify the object. Older learners will enjoy a more difficult close-up photograph, acting as detectives to find the answer (see, for example, Figure 3.2).

Observational activities provide plenty of scope for exploration and questioning. Learners enjoy a challenge and 'mystery parcels' offers the opportunity to develop observation using a variety of senses and the development of vocabulary. An object can be wrapped in newspaper – a little like the party game 'pass the parcel'. Once it is wrapped, learners can be asked to feel the parcel and to note any words used to describe it. After a short time they can be asked to try to identify the object from their observations, then to unwrap the object and note down further words to describe the object. Alternatively, an object could be placed in a shoebox, or smaller items, such as paperclips, a magnet or a piece of Plasticene, could be placed in a matchbox.

Observational skills can also be developed through the use of simple games. 'Feely bags' are popular in many classrooms. Variations on the theme of 'Kim's game' (discussed in Chapter 9) provide learners with the opportunity to look at a tray full of objects including a range of different items made of different materials, e.g. balloon, plastic spoon, fabric and rubber ball (fewer for younger learners, more for older learners) for a few minutes, before having to recall what is on the tray. This game, as well as developing memory, can be extended to differentiate not only what the object is, but learners can also be asked to recall finer details, for example, what colour the object is, how many wheels it has, and finer details about the wheel, such as how many spokes it has. Learners can play the 'yes/no' game where one child secretly chooses one item from the tray and others ask questions to try to identify the object. This will require

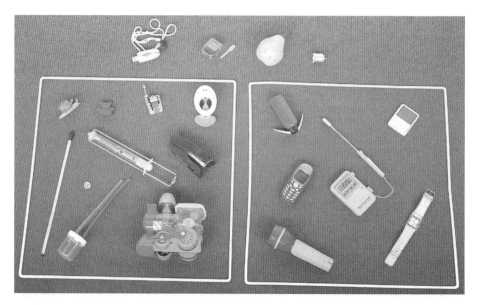

Figure 3.3   Photograph of grouped objects. Which group do the four objects belong in?

learners to think about the detail of an object and/or what it is made of. Some variations might include hard/soft, shiny/dull, natural/human-made. From a planning perspective, differentiation is 'built in' and is achieved by outcome.

Sorting and Classifying

Being asked to sort and classify provided objects naturally leads to seeing similarities and differences between objects. Sorting and classifying is also fundamental to science. Learners need to be given many opportunities, starting from observation using all their senses, and from their earliest days in school, to develop systematically the skills of sorting and classifying. At the Foundation Stage and Key Stage 1, this mainly involves sorting based on gross features. Can learners sort into two groups, three groups or four groups? A variation on this theme could be that the teacher sorts a group of objects and challenges the learners to state which criterion has been used to classify. A further development could be where the teacher provides objects sorted into two groups and provides other objects for learners to add to one of the groups. Learners then need to explain why the new object belongs in the chosen group (Figure 3.3).

Learners group from an early age, but are not able to give reasons for doing so. Learners say that things just 'go together' instead of having the same characteristic. It is tempting to think that older learners need not practise these basic skills, but they too need opportunities to notice more detail and to look for more sophisticated patterns within and between objects. Therefore older learners should be challenged to make finer observations of everyday and more unusual objects.

Basic sorting not only leads to classification but, in itself, helps to develop learners' observation skills by asking them to examine detail to find out which groups they belong to. Observation in this context leads learners to notice patterns, for example that all seashells have similarities and are made of the same material, but that differences between shells are often substantial. Finer observation of detail may reveal differences between other things that are basically 'the same', such as rocks, or a natural seasonal change like the discoloration of leaves in the autumn.

Learners' Observations

Experience suggests that observations are frequently influenced by past experiences and therefore learners' observations are often not what might be expected. Learners will often observe what they think they can see, but actually it is often what is stored in their memory. Such observations are frequently 'contaminated' by their previous experience. For some learners, observation is important because they may be being asked to look closely at some objects for the first time. Young learners can often surprise adults by what they notice and it is important that their observations are not dismissed as being irrelevant. Young learners make sense of things based on previous experience and therefore it should not be surprising when they appear to make what adults might think are irrelevant observations. In some ways, young learners' observations can be very limited, while often being influenced by other things in their real world, such as storybooks and other aspects of popular culture like videos and cartoons. Johnson (2005, p.33) says that children's creative approach to observation needs to be encouraged and she says that children's drawings often show their 'observation skills and creativity' and that these 'creative additions' indicate wider powers of observation (ibid., p.35). Furthermore, the way in which this manifests itself in learners' drawings often differs according to gender. Girls tend to include more 'touchy feely' additions while boys generally will be more imaginative in their additions. However, there is an obvious tension here because on the one hand we want to encourage learners to be creative, but on the other we want them to make accurate observations of things in their environment.

What Do Learners Notice?

The three observational drawings of fish shown in Figure 3.4 are all drawings of the same trout drawn on the same day by 7-year-old learners. The fish was placed on a white tray in the middle of a large table and learners were placed around the table and asked to draw the fish. The quality of the drawings varies enormously; fish 1 shows much immaturity in both observational and drawing skills, but indicates features observed by the child and reproduced on the drawing. Fish 2 has a noticeable head feature that is more reminiscent of a turtle, rather than a fish. Many people assessing fish 3 choose this as the best drawing of a fish, which it is; however, the drawing is typical of one that draws

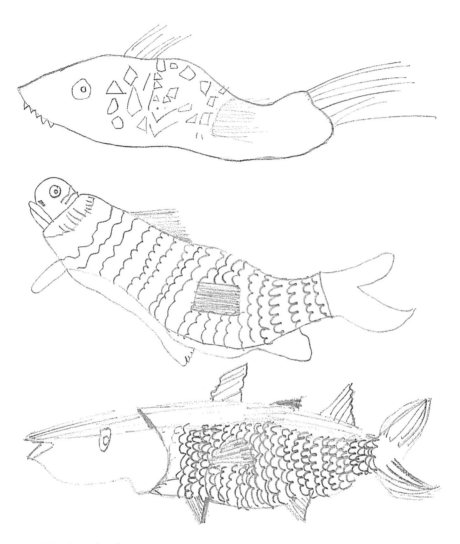

Figure 3.4   Fish drawings

more from memory of pictures of fish than from observation of the fish on the table. The role of the teacher here is very important, as learners need to be asked regularly what is being noticed to enable them to discriminate fine detail.

On the other hand, the drawings of various small creatures, drawn by very young learners, indicate that they have been influenced by remembered images of the creatures from books of fiction or other aspects of popular culture. In particular, it is noticeable that both the drawings of ladybirds have faces drawn on them (Figure 3.5). A drawing of a crane fly, while showing some very good observed features, provided a more creative impression rather than the observed creature. One boy drew a crane fly that had almost fairy-like qualities and the ladybirds, drawn by girls, have been given human-like characteristics. These are typical of young learners' drawings of real things in their environment.

Clearly, from a science point of view, while wanting to encourage creativity, it would be preferable that the drawings focused on observable features and

Figure 3.5   Drawings of ladybirds showing human-like characteristics

did not include fanciful features perhaps influenced by learners' literature and other media. One further problem here is that teachers will regularly praise highly such drawings becasue of their artistic, creative content rather than their close observations.

Other activities that do not require such intense teacher input, within the context of life processes and living things, could include learners sorting picture cards or model animals into groups. This leads directly on to classification of living things. Younger learners will sort things familiar to themselves in various categories, for example whether they fly, walk or swim; alternatively they may group the 'scary' animals and the 'friendly' animals. Older learners should be more able to group animals into scientific groups and, if not, should be challenged to do so. An activity like this can assess the extent to which learners understand, for example, the vertebrate groups. Experience tells us that many adults as well as learners will group amphibians (frogs, toads, salamanders and newts) with reptiles (lizards, snakes, et.). While both groups have some similar features, there are major differences which need to be identified. Talking to learners and students in training it is clear that they become more, not less, confused about animal groups as they get older. This needs to be dealt with at a simple level at the primary stage.

There are a number of misconceptions relating to animal groups that are commonly held by learners and many adults. For example, young learners will often be confused because, although it can fly, a bat is a mammal. Similarly, a penguin can be confusing because although it is a bird, it does not fly in the air. Dolphins are often considered to be fish rather than mammals, and the difference between reptiles and amphibians is not often clear. Amphibians have soft, damp bodies and start their lives in water, whereas reptiles tend to have scaly skins. Frogs, toad, newts and salamanders are amphibians, lizards, snakes, turtles, crocodiles and alligators are reptiles. The confusion arises because newts and salamanders look like some lizards and many reptiles are amphibious, that is, they spend time in water and on land. Many adults are not clear about the difference between vertebrates, those animals with backbones, and invertebrates, those without backbones. In particular, worms, snakes and some lizards, such as slow-worms, are confused because at first glance they have similar features. Where invertebrates are concerned, many individuals have problems in relation to 'insects' where in everyday usage this term often means all small creatures such as spiders, millipedes, etc., whereas the term 'insect', in science, relates specifically only to those creatures that have six legs, a thorax, a head and an abdomen.

Using models that are not made to scale, common in many early years' classrooms, also might lead to misconceptions with younger learners. It also needs to be borne in mind that sometimes even identification books can help to promote misconceptions. Teachers and parents need to be aware of the possibility that some identification books, even if entitled 'Insects', may well include animals of other subgroups, for example, spiders, molluscs and crustaceans.

Making and Using Keys

Basic sorting leads to classification. Learners of all ages need to be able to use classification keys: even Foundation Stage learners can be introduced to simple keys made up by their teacher or by older learners especially for their younger peers. Using keys can help learners to become less confused about animal groups. This is one good reason for including them in teaching in the primary classroom. Use of keys should start off simply, based on a very few different objects with very different characteristics. Older learners need to be introduced progressively to more complex keys. The oldest and most able primary learners can be expected to be able to make keys. Once again, learners should be introduced to this by being given fewer and very different objects and then asked to draw up a list of characteristics for each object. They can then be asked to make up a simple branching key. Coins could provide a good starting point for this. Once made, learners could swap keys to see if they work.

Other Aspects of Observation

It is important to remember that observation in science includes all the senses and therefore it is appropriate for learners to be asked to identify things using other senses than sight. Learners could undertake a 'senses survey' where they are asked to notice things deliberately placed in the room, for example, a fan blowing at foot level; did they notice? A smell in the room, for example, perfume or sliced onions revealed at a certain point in a session. There could be things to feel when blindfold, such as a teddy bear or rough sandpaper, and things to listen to, for example, at what level of loudness can learners first identify a tune well known to them? Can they identify taped noises, of a tap running, a clock ticking, etc.?

Observation is very important when learners are carrying out practical work. Obviously it is important that data collected within an illustrative activity or

Figure 3.6   Salt dissolving in water over time

an investigation is accurate and reliable. Learners need to be able to read scales on a thermometer or Newton meter with accuracy as inaccuracy can lead to much wasted time. Accurate observations of change, over time, is also crucial to the outcome of an investigation and to what learners learn from the experience:

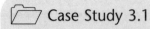

Case Study 3.1

A class of Year 4 children were attempting to separate four mixtures. Included in the mixtures was one of gravel and salt. Having successfully separated the gravel from the salt using a sieve, one group added the remaining salt to water. In response to the adult helper's question, one child explained that they did this because the salt would dissolve in the water. The learner showed the resulting cloudy-looking liquid to the adult and said the salt had dissolved. The group then went straight to the next task without another thought about the salt water. However, their attention was re-focused on the salt water mixture by the adult, who realised that something unexpected had been observed: the salt solution should be clear, not cloudy. This led to further exploration and close observation by the group. A teaspoon of salt was added to about 100ml of water and stirred. The group watched what was happening in the beaker and noticed that at first the mixture looked cloudy and it was only after a number of seconds that the liquid became clear. At this point the adult introduced the word 'transparent' and emphasised the need for the liquid to be transparent to be able to say that the solute (in this instance the salt) had dissolved. Facinated by the change over time, the learners went on to take photographs of the changes in the water as the salt dissolved (see Fig. 3.6). Had the adult helper not taken action in this way, the children may well have continued to think that solutions look cloudy.

Summary

Observing is the skill of absorbing all the information about the things around. Learners need to be encouraged to notice fine detail and go beyond what they expect to see. Learners should develop the ability to distinguish what is relevant and what is not. They should be given the opportunity to record observations in a variety of ways including talking, writing or through their drawings.

The teacher's role in developing observation skills is not to be the fount of all knowledge. Rather, the teacher should enable learners to see with 'new' eyes. The teacher can do this by carefully structuring opportunities for the development of observation skills. Plenty of resources need to be provided; materials need to be selected carefully. Learners need the opportunity to share their observations with others and need to be questioned about what they are noticing.

Further Reading

Harlen, W. and Symington, D. (1985) 'Helping Children to Observe', in Harlen, W. (ed.) *Primary Science: Taking the Plunge*. London: Heinemann.

Rix, C. and McSorley, J. (1999) 'An investigation into the role that school-based interactive science centres may play in the education of primary-aged children', *International Journal Science Education* 21: 6, 577–93.

4

Raising and Analysing Questions and Use of Secondary Sources

Judith Roden

Introduction

Chapter 3 explained how observation, as a fundamental skill, could lead learners naturally to seeing patterns and sorting into groups, leading to classification. Following on directly from Chapter 3, this chapter will focus more particularly on asking questions, which, along with measurement and classification, are often neglected aspects of scientific enquiry. The nature of learners' questions and how teachers can provide a role model will be explored. The chapter will also provide an analysis of teachers' and learners' questions that form the basis for productive learning at an appropriate level in the primary classroom, with examples of the questions that learners ask and how these can be responded to.

Learners Raising Questions within Statutory Requirements

In the Early Years Foundation Stage, there is an increasing expectation, building on pre-school learning, that learners will ask questions. The *Curriculum Guidance for the Foundation Stage* advises teachers to encourage children to ask questions about why things happen and how things work (QCA, 2000, pp.88–9). Learners are also expected to 'learn to investigate, be curious ... pose questions, and use reference skills' (ibid.). Learners should also be encouraged to suggest solutions to, and answers for, their own questions. Here the role of the teacher is crucial in providing a good role model when interacting with learners playing with and exploring materials. This is particularly important when they are exploring materials at first hand in order to place them into simple groups as a precursor to classification.

During the primary years questioning forms part of the 'planning' at both Key Stages. At Key Stage 1 learners should be encouraged to extend the type of questions asked, to include, for example, 'How?', 'Why?', 'What will happen if … ?' (DfEE, 1999, p.16) and decide how they might find answers to them. They should also be encouraged to 'use first-hand experience and simple information sources to answer questions' (ibid.). At Key Stage 2, naturally, the requirement is more demanding as learners are expected to 'ask questions that can be investigated scientifically and decide how to find answers [and to] consider what sources of information, including first-hand experience and a range of other sources, they will use to answer questions' (DfEE, 1999, p.21).

While in the Early Years Foundation Stage learners will need help to find the answers to questions, by Key Stage 1 they should be encouraged to try to find their own answers, unaided, using a variety of books and Internet sources, as well as being guided by the teacher to try to find answers to some questions by hands-on practical work. The role of the teacher here is to listen to learners' ideas and to modify and develop them into something that can be investigated. Building on this, Key Stage 2 learners should be able to access a wider range of sources to find answers to their 'Why?' and other questions and should be regularly challenged to discuss whether or not their questions can be answered by practical investigation rather than merely the use of secondary sources.

Traditionally, some teachers have viewed learners' questions about science as a threat both to their authority and to their own knowledge and understanding, rather than as an aspect of learning to be encouraged. While there is more understanding now, it is still true that some teachers are afraid of their learners' questions on a subject they still feel less confident about. Frequently this was due to teachers' perceptions that they should be able to answer all the questions asked of them, reflecting a now misguided view of the teacher as the 'fount of all knowledge'. This has led, perhaps unconsciously, to questioning being discouraged, although realistically, given the vastness of science, most teachers and even the most eminent of scientists cannot be expected to hold the answers to all the questions learners might ask.

Although there is an expectation for teachers to focus on learners' questions and to help them to develop their ability to raise questions, in practice this rarely happens. Teachers often argue that learners do not ask questions, and those that do, ask questions that they find difficulty in knowing how to deal with. This is in part due to the unsophisticated way in which the questions are expressed and partly because many questions are difficult to answer directly. However, this is not a good enough reason to avoid questioning because, when learners are given the opportunity to explore and investigate for themselves, questions are often an important by-product.

Providing a good role model here is crucial. Learners of any age will not ask questions if they are not encouraged to look closely at things or to ask questions about them. Neither will they make progress in the types of questions to ask if the adults around them do not ask the kinds of questions that can lead to higher-order thinking skills. 'Wait time' in science teaching is still an area that could be developed further, with the time between asking the question and expecting an answer still painfully inadequate. When learners are given more time and the original question is not reworded or moved on to the next learner, they have to begin to think for themselves and often astound teachers with their understanding.

Extending the type and function of questions is also necessary. *Application questions*, i.e. those where the learners have to think about the knowledge in a new setting, help to promote and extend thinking far more than low-level knowledge questions in which the learners have a 50 per cent chance of being right: for example, 'Is salt a solid or a liquid?' compared with: 'If aliens landed on earth and wanted to know what a solid was, how would you describe the properties of a solid so that they understood?'

Analytical questions require learners to discuss how things are the same and different or what are the major causes of the event. For example:

Q: 'Does sugar dissolve?'
A: 'No.'

can be replaced with

Q: 'What are the differences between melting and dissolving?'
A: 'Melting is where the stuff changes shape, it goes runny and watery and a bit melty, but dissolving the stuff will go into the water so you cannot see it. Melting you can see but dissolving you can not.' (Joseph, Year 6)

Synthesis questions start from the premise that learners can think for themselves, and link ideas together. For example, a group of Year 6 learners were looking at 'instant snow' which expands when water is added. They thought originally that the powder would dissolve, so were rather surprised by their observations. They thought that if you added more water it would dissolve and, so, a small amount of 'instant snow' powder was added to a large amount of water. It was still possible to see the granules.

Q: 'Based on your idea that when materials dissolve they are too small to see, can you explain if this is an example of dissolving?' (Teacher)
A: 'You can still see the small bits of the stuff it is floating in the water. But if you add more water it will probably dissolve.' (Brett, Year 6)
Q: 'Do you agree with Brett?' (Teacher)
A: 'You can see the small bits but adding water will not make a difference it would have done it by now if it was going to. I think you could put it on a radiator in the sun and get it back so it's like dissolving because it will evaporate.' (Joseph, Year 6)

Synthesis questions are ones that prompt learners to see links and enable the teacher to plan the next steps in their learning as a result of expressing their ideas verbally. Synthesis questions are very helpful and are typified as 'So, based on this fact, what would your conclusions be?' type questions.

It is also important to allow opportunities for learners to experience *evaluative questions*, which enable them to rank statements. For example, using the idea cards in Figure 4.1, the learners had to decide which definition they agreed most with, or make up one of their own.

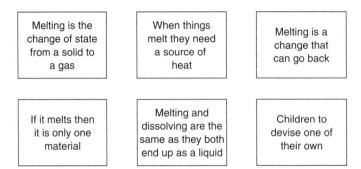

Figure 4.1   Evaluative questions

It is also important to include some *interpretive questions*, which require an opinion from the learners, a useful strategy for responses, which are scientifically inaccurate. So when one learner suggested, 'Dissolving is when it disappears or disintegrates' (Libby, Year 6), this response was used as a question to the class, 'Why would you agree with this statement?' thus allowing thinking time and responses from the learners, with the teacher taking the role to move learning forward rather than being controlling.

Whatever range of strategies are used there is safety in numbers for learners. Using talking pairs is helpful, but ensuring that the pairs are changed every two weeks is vital. Linking 'Talk pairs' into 'Thoughtful fours' (two pairs of learners asked to consider ideas in a thoughtful way) can ensure a range of ideas are raised. Although calling out and putting hands up occurs in some classrooms, this practice means that only a few learners have to 'do the work'. The hands-up strategy also leaves the problem of the learners who do not have to take part. Traditional questioning with hands up is found to be detrimental to the development of thinking and is a type of neural pruning. If the brain is not used effectively its ability to make links is reduced. But when 'wait time' is increased, response partners are used and the quality of questioning is improved, learners make thoughtful responses and become more involved in their learning. Neural branching is an outcome of effective questioning.

Using Learners' Questions as a Starting Point

Teachers should aim to use learners' questions as often as possible for a number of varied reasons. Questioning as a process skill is an important part of the scientific process. As Smith and Peacock (1995, p.14) state, 'learning to ask good questions is an essential ingredient for science' and, in the long term, a scientifically literate person needs to be an effective questioner, someone who can use their knowledge and understanding alongside the ability and confidence to ask the right question at the right time. Primary-aged learners are living in an uncertain world where being able to question the world around them is increasingly important. Therefore it is important to encourage learners' questions within formal education today.

Learners' Questions

Pre-school children naturally raise many 'why' questions. This is typified in the book *Why* (Camp and Ross, 2000), a story of Lily and her father, who becomes increasingly exasperated trying to answer Lily's incessant 'why' questions. Experience suggests that 'why' questions are asked when children do not understand something, or when they need either to gain further information or to extend their knowledge of a familiar subject, or sometimes merely to gain attention from adults.

Although 'why' questions are important for developing learners' knowledge and understanding of science, they are not the most important for providing opportunities to develop science process skills. Starting from learners' own questions can provide some ownership of their own learning and, consequently, can be a terrific motivator. It is crucial that they do not merely undertake practical activities to reinforce existing ideas or to illustrate a concept. While illustrative activities are important, it is also most important to provide opportunities for practical exploration and investigation of things with which they are not yet familiar. Merely asking questions that learners already know the answers to could lead to disaffection, characterised by unwelcome questions such as 'Why are we doing this?' However, if investigations are based on learners' own questions then the outcome will not be known before the exploration, research or investigation begins. Furthermore, learners' questions can also be a focus for formative assessment, not only to assess what they know or, more importantly, do not know, but also to provide an opportunity for teachers to assess the quality of their question-raising ability.

Answering Learners' Questions

Learners do need to ask questions to obtain information and to clarify unclear thinking. Many of the 'why' questions they ask can be easily answered by reference to textbooks set at the appropriate level. Children are fascinated by questions that ask, for example, about the tallest tree, the shortest man, etc. However, merely providing learners with the 'correct' answer will rarely provide the long-term solution. Clearly, though, it would not be realistic, or appropriate, to expect teachers never to answer their questions and teachers need to use their professional judgement when learners ask questions. Before directly answering a question, teachers need to consider if doing so is in the best interest of the learner. Sometimes, as discussed above, it is appropriate to throw the question over to their peers, as other learners can often offer an answer that is set at the appropriate level using more learner-centred language, or that provides a new slant that will enable more discussion to occur.

Instead of always being provided with the answer, learners need to be taught to ask their own questions as a way of obtaining information and understanding in science. Learners also need to recognise that for some questions, there is no known answer, and that there are various ways of finding out the answers to different kinds of questions. Older learners also need to learn how to make their initial questions into ones that can be investigated so they can find an answer by practical scientific enquiry. In order to learn this skill, learners need time and the opportunity, built into their learning time, to consider what sorts of questions are suitable for answering by practical enquiry. Some ideas for developing this further are provided in Chapter 5.

By helping children to clarify, qualify and refine the question, the teacher's role is actually enhanced. Throwing the problem back to the learners, asking 'What makes you ask that?' or 'What do you mean by that?', may well lead to more meaningful, longer-term learning than directly answering the question when the provided answer may or may not match the understanding of the learner. It is a common occurrence, even in adulthood, to be put off asking further questions because the answer to an initial question, even if accurate, was not understood. Answering learners' questions at the correct level, with differentiation, is a very difficult instructional skill and, more often than not, it is probably in the best interests of the learner if they are required to find out for themselves.

Helping Learners to Raise Questions

In order to help learners to develop their question-raising ability, teachers need to listen to their questions, analysing them to try to discover the reason for the question and whether or not they can be answered by practical enquiry. One of the most useful ways of promoting the questions that can lead to further practical enquiry is to provide learners with the opportunity to explore and observe some objects, using all the senses (where appropriate). Older learners can be given a simple resource and asked to ask questions about it. One Year 6 class provided with a potato as a stimulus raised 98 different questions. The teacher said that the questions ranged from 'Where did the original potato come from?' to 'How can we grow a potato?' So successful is this strategy that it is almost possible to base a whole term's cross-curricular work on the questions raised – very much in keeping with the current trend towards more cross-curricular work! While the same range of questions may not be possible for all starting points, experience suggests that the latent potential of learners raising their own questions may well be enormous. One strategy that helps learners to raise questions is the use of a question hand (Figure 4.2).

Learners were provided with some white powder (instant snow) in a transparent plastic cup and asked to think of questions they could ask about this and write them on their first hand. Then they were asked to add water to the powder and to observe what happened and to ask some more questions on their second hand. All learners asked 10 questions, many of which could have been answered using a practical activity. It was interesting that the quality of the questions improved greatly after the water was added.

Learners Looking at Small Animals
There is often a tendency for teachers to ask learners to research, prior to their exploration, the sorts of animals they may encounter in their local environment.

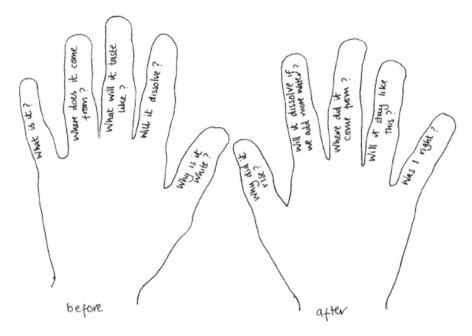

Figure 4.2 The question hand

The argument used to justify this strategy is that learners will then be more informed about the animals they are likely to encounter before finding them. However, while important, knowing the name of an animal is not the most important reason for observing them. Preparing learners in this way is tantamount to putting the cart before the horse in terms of learning because, inevitably, they are likely to notice those features that they have been prepared to notice, rather than observing features in an open-minded way (see Chapter 3). Learners' questioning ability and their knowledge and understanding of small animals can be extended if they are challenged to notice similarities and differences between animals while observing them, then they will not only begin to appreciate the wide diversity of living things, but will also develop the scientific skill of classification of invertebrates. This will be particularly so if they are encouraged to use classification keys to identify the animals they come across.

When learners are given the opportunity to observe a number of small animals it is almost impossible to stop them from asking questions about them. If they are asked to observe collected material for a few minutes, then to view the individuals, one at a time, in a viewer, they become fascinated. It is easy, for learners working in pairs, to record their questions, either in writing or on tape, and then to seek answers to their questions. This strategy is particularly motivating because learners themselves have ownership of the questions they ask and require little formal input from the teacher.

One reason why this activity can be such a good vehicle for raising questions is that learners will immediately compare the animal to themselves and, among the many 'why' questions, there will be more productive questions such as:

- What is it?
- What does it eat?
- How does it feed?
- How many legs has it got?
- What are the feelers for?
- Does it have eyes?
- Is it a boy or a girl?
- Is this a baby one of these?

Teachers can prompt learners, through questioning, into noticing missed features that are important to learning. Then learners can choose some of the questions that they would really like to be answered either through looking again more closely, using secondary sources or by setting up a practical situation to try to find the answer to the question. While consulting secondary sources looking for the answers to specific questions, learners invariably not only find answers to questions that they had not even asked, but also begin to realise that some questions cannot easily be answered.

Of course, teachers need to provide a variety of resources and also to be aware themselves of which questions should be answered in a practical way, for example: 'What does the animal eat?', 'Under what conditions does it prefer to live?' or 'How far does the animal travel in five minutes?' etc. Teachers also need to know how these could be carried out practically, then, without giving too much information, they should scaffold learning so they can go about finding the answers to their questions. For a successful outcome, secondary resources set at an appropriate level need to be readily available. It is important here to be aware that some well-known and recently published materials may unintentionally transmit misconceptions. For example, one book of insects contains spiders and another aimed at the primary age range has a large heading of 'Insects' on the cover with a much smaller heading of 'and other small creatures that live in the soil', with large pictures of a variety of groups of small animals on both the back and front cover of the book.

One of the best things about approaching this topic in an open-ended 'learner directed' way, starting with questions, is that it is highly likely that the questions asked by learners will follow curriculum guidance. Not only are learners introduced to the wide variety of living things by using such an approach, but also they are highly likely to explore the seven life processes of living things, namely, movement, reproduction, sensitivity, nutrition, respiration, growth and, though not in the statutory National Curriculum at Key Stages 1 or 2, excretion – a topic very much of interest to children! In working in this way, learners are very motivated and this suggests that the teaching style adopted has an effect on learners' learning, which is not seen with a list drawn up by the teacher. This approach still requires intervention by the teacher, not to direct learning in a formal way, but to ask the questions that learners have not asked themselves.

Bubbles

Playing with bubbles is a common play activity both inside the early years classroom and outside. Bubbles fascinate learners of all ages. They provide a

Pupils' observations or statements	Teacher questions
	What have you noticed about the bubble?
The bubble is coloured	What colour is a bubble? How many colours can you see? What do the colours remind you of?
The bubble is round	Are all bubbles the same shape? What shape is a bubble? What shape is the bubble as you blow through the frame? Can you blow a square bubble?
The bubbles float	What happens if you use different size bubble frames? Can you make it touch the ceiling? Will it stay in the air forever? How long can you get it to stay off the ground? What do you think is inside the bubble? How is it different from the bubble mixture? Does it float up or down? Why do you think it moved that way? How did you make it move that way?
I can blow a big bubble	What happens to the size of the bubble when you blow slowly? What happens to the size of the bubble when you blow quickly? In which ways are big and small bubbles the same and in which ways are they different?
The bubble popped	What is the shape of the popped bubble? How long did the bubble last? Can you count how many seconds the bubble lasted before it popped? If the bubble was made out of a different material would it still pop?
Look, two bubbles bumped into each other	What happens to the shape of bubbles when two bubbles join together? How many bubbles can you make stick together? Magnets attract some metals. Do you think this is the same? What shape can you see inside the bubble?
I can see reflections	What can you see in the reflections? Are the reflections the right way up? Can your bubble make a shadow? How do a shadow and a reflection differ?
It is dripping	What words can you use to describe the bubble now? Could you get a dry bubble?

Figure 4.3   Teacher questions to aid observation and promote simple investigations

wonderful starting point for simple investigations arising out of observation. The beauty of using bubbles as a starting point for simple observational activities is that a whole series of activities based on simple observation can be completed in a few minutes. When starting with all resources for exploration, it is important that teachers have explored the possibilities for themselves, before the activity is carried out with learners. It is also important to note that the learning outcomes here relate to process skills objectives and not, except incidentally, to those relating to knowledge and understanding.

Observing and Raising Questions about Bubbles

The example in Figure 4.3 shows the types of questions that teachers can use not only to encourage further observation, but also to model the kinds of questions that can be investigated practically. Initially learners should be provided with a pot of bubble mixture and bubble wands of various shapes and sizes. Once they have begun to explore blowing bubbles, the possibilities for simple investigations arising out of frequently unstated questions are almost endless. The most important thing here is for the teacher not to ask questions too soon, or too quickly. Initially, it is better to watch what learners are doing and to listen to what they are saying and to take the questioning from them, rather than to have a predetermined list of questions that *have* to be delivered. Observations and explorations need to be built upon, rather than superimposing a set diet of activity on the learners.

After just a few minutes learners can share their observations with the rest of the class. Some will have focused on some aspects and not noticed others. Sharing observations here allows a much wider number of observations and simple investigations to be undertaken in a relatively short time.

Progression in Learners Raising Questions

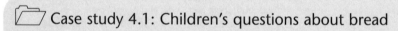

Case study 4.1: Children's questions about bread

Bread is a very good starting point for scientific investigations and has the additional attraction of providing a multicultural dimension. What follows is a case study account of the response of four learners, two girls and two boys from each of Years R, 2, 4 and 6. All learners were provided with the same starting point, a variety of 'breads' from around the world to explore, to observe using all the senses and to raise questions about. The breads provided were:

- Baquette: typical French bread
- Pitta Bread: unleavened bread that can be split open to hold a filling
- Chapatti: flat 'bread' with obvious herbs within it
- Naan bread: leavened Indian bread in a flattened tear-drop shape
- Mediterranean roll: a very colourful, rich bread with identifiable pieces of olive and tomato within it
- Stay fresh white bread: 'long life'
- Ciabatta: flattish Italian bread made with olive oil
- Wholemeal brown bread: traditional sliced brown bread

Initially all learners from each year group were asked what they noticed about the different breads at the exploration stage. If necessary they were then prompted with the following questions:

- What do you think it tastes like?
- What does it smell like?

- What does it look like?
- What might you eat it with?
- Where do you think it comes from?
- When would you eat it?
- Do you know what sort of bread it is?

Learners were asked to:

- Look at the bread
- Think of any words to describe the bread
- Choose one type of bread to draw
- Ask any questions about the bread (the question hand was used again).

All learners were most interested in the Mediterranean bread, the chapatti and the naan bread. Of all the breads, the Mediterranean bread was the least familiar and white bread and wholemeal bread the most familiar.

Pupils' observations of Mediterranean bread, and activities that could follow

Year Group	Children's Observations	Activities that could follow the observations
Foundation stage	Tended not to comment about the bread, but their observational drawings suggested that they had noticed 'bits' of black pieces of olive and red pieces of tomato within the bread.	The 'bits' could have been taken from the bread, put in piles and weights of each could be compared using simple scales, to find the proportion of each.
Year 2	Looks like a currant bun with cracks on it. It looks like it has raisins in it. It tastes fruity – very yummy. Learners thought it came from a bakery in Dover.	Comparison of the olives and tomatoes with raisins by sight, touch and taste to see if the learners' ideas were correct. Finding out what was in the bread by comparison of simple possible ingredients.
Year 4	Jane noticed that the bread 'smells like garlic' and noticed herbs and 'fruit' in it. She thought that its texture was 'quite squidgey' and tasted tomatoey like pasta sauce and came originally from Italy.	It was interesting that Jane compared the taste of the bread to her experience of other food. She was trying to make sense of her observations. The smell of the bread could have been compared to a clove of garlic and a range of herbs used for baking.

(Continued)

(Continued)

Year 6	Mandy thought it had fruit inside and that the texture was hard, on the outside, but 'squidgey and lumpy on the inside'. She did not like the taste, describing it as disgusting because she detected the smell of garlic and herbs with the bread. Mandy commented that it was difficult to describe the smell.	The Year 6 learners were much more sophisticated in their previous experience of foods and were able to correctly identify a number of tastes presented to them in the bread. They also had more understanding of the origin of various foodstuffs. However, they tended not to ask questions that could be investigated.
	Egan thought the bread probably came from Italy. Sam thought it looked brown and bumpy and that it felt hard and lumpy. He thought it tasted like a pasta sauce and thought that the bread came from Italy because pasta a comes from Italy. Tim thought the bread looked like a fruit cake, smelled like tomato purée, was hard and tasted a bit like pizza and came from Italy.	Again though, these learners could have explored further the proportion of ingredients and compared tastes of herbs that might have been in the bread. Acting like detectives, before looking on the bread packet.

Questions children asked about the bread

Inevitably, a number of questions were asked by learners of all years that were not particularly productive in terms of leading to further observation or investigation in science. Examples of these included 'Where did the bread come from?' 'What is the name of the bread?' 'Have you ever been to the country where this bread comes from?' However, other questions were potentially more useful.

Questions leading to further practical work

Year	Question	Questions that could lead to further practical work
Year R	Notices the 'bits' in the bread	How many different 'bits' are there in the bread? What are the 'bits' in the bread?
Year 2	How is the bread made?	Making bread using the ingredients listed on the packet.

Year 4	Why does the 'stay fresh' bread always stay fresh'?	How long does 'stay fresh' bread stay fresh? Looking on the packet for the 'use by' date. Comparing bread packets to find out what ingredient helped to keep the bread fresher for longer.
		Setting up a practical situation (taking care to do this safely) to find out which bread, e.g. 'stay fresh', ordinary white bread and wholemeal bread, stays freshest for longest.
		Making bread using ingredients listed on packets (where possible).
		Omitting single ingredients systematically to find out what difference this makes to the bread.
	Why did the Mediterranean bread taste like 'Domino's' pizza?	What ingredients give the bread its characteristic smell? Comparing herbs in pots to smell of bread to try and determine the ingredients.
	Why has the naan bread got 'bits' in it?	What would the naan bread taste like without the 'bits' in it? Find out what the bits are, making naan bread without the 'bits'.
	Why is the baguette my favourite?	Survey of children's preferences of the breads under study.
Year 6	Why do you like it?	Survey of the reasons why learners like different breads.
	Where does it come from?	Answers found by consulting secondary sources.
	What is special about it?	Comparing breads by further observation and looking at lists of ingredients from packets or recipe books.
	Why is it called chapatti?	Research of secondary sources.
	What does it smell of?	Comparison of the smell of different breads.
	What colour is it? How would you describe it?	Describing the colour of different breads. Asking learners to describe bread.
	How do you think it was made?	Looking up recipes and trying to make the bread.

(Continued)

(Continued)

While most of the learners involved in the case study knew what a question was, they were not very good at raising investigative questions. However, some questions could be derived from their spontaneous questions and some of these could lead to further observation or investigative work.

Summary

Learners ask a wide variety of questions, but some of these are not as useful in promoting scientific enquiry as others. Observation works to encourage questioning because learners are starting with things they notice and in which they are interested. The teacher's role in this process is to encourage observation, to ask learners what they have noticed and to clarify questions.

Finally, it is important to know when and how to intervene when learners ask questions. It is pertinent to note at this point that in the Early Years teachers are warned that 'giving the game away' too early during an activity may limit the depth of learners' learning; telling learners before they have a chance to experience the 'eureka moment' provides information, but prevents the development of investigative skills (QCA, 2000, p.83). This message is true also of all teaching in science and the implication of this may well be far-reaching for many teachers in the primary classroom.

Further Reading

Chin, C. and Brown, D. 'Student-generated questions: a meaningful aspect of learning in science', *International Journal of Science Education* 24: 5, 521–49.

Harlen, W. (2006), 'Teachers' and chidren's questioning', in Harlen, W. (ed.) *ASE Guide to Primary Science Education*. Hatfield: The Association of Science Education.

Harlen, W., Macro, C., Reed, K. and Schilling, M. (2003) 'Teachers' questions and responses to children's questions Module 3', in *Making Progress in Primary Science*. London: Routledge Falmer.

5

Scientific Enquiry

Hellen Ward

Introduction

This chapter will highlight the difference between illustrative and investigative activities. The procedures involved in investigating an idea will be developed in sequence and illustrated with learners' work where appropriate. Some suggested complete investigations will be provided and the chapter will conclude with a reminder that the fair test is only one type of investigation.

The Importance of Scientific Enquiry

The focus of science teaching has most recently centred upon the knowledge and understanding of science at the expense of investigative and illustrative processes, due in part to the emphasis upon high status national tests. As a result many learners receive a very bland and boring diet of science involving comprehension tasks. Recently concerns were being raised about the overemphasis of content at the expense of skills and enjoyment (Wellcome, 2005, p.3). This lack of investigative approaches has also been commented upon in a number of forums from parliamentary reports (2003), OfSTED publications (Ofsted/HMI, 2002; 2003; 2004) and the professional press. Time pressure, a testing arrangement that appeared to favour what was 'easy to test' rather than 'what is science', together with the introduction of 'the National Primary Strategies', have all contributed to the current position. Whilst in the first edition of this book it was hoped that the changes to the tests initiated in 2003 might help to refocus science teaching, there has been no real evidence of this in practice.

Investigative work is more than any activity that involves equipment and practical tasks. Figure 5.1 denotes the stages of scientific enquiry. It can be seen

1. Selection of the global question*
2. Identification of the independent variables
3. Thinking of how to measure/observe the outcome (dependent variable)
4. Question generation
5. Selecting the equipment and deciding how to use it
6. Deciding what might happen (making a prediction) if needed*
7. Data collection methods – type and amount of data to be collected*
8. Making observations and measurements
9. Recording and evaluating the data (reliability)
10. Interpreting the data
11. Drawing conclusions
12. Evaluating the process*

*Using secondary sources of information can occur at a number of points. It will differ according to the investigation as well as age of learners, but is an important part of the process.

Figure 5.1   The stages of scientific enquiry

that there are many steps, and when undertaking an investigation the learners will follow and be involved in all the steps. In illustrative work the teacher will undertake steps 1–5. This is perhaps why learners make so many predictions as this is the first part of the process where they can be involved. Basic skill lessons focus on only one step at a time, as discussed in detail in Chapter 2.

The term 'investigation' is used explicitly for activities which require learners to think and make choices about 'what to vary' and 'what to measure'. It is this choice that is important as it enables the learners to plan their own work. In investigative work learners plan by selecting the variable (factor) they will change and then deciding how to measure and record the effect of the changes. The learners then carry out the whole process of investigating their own idea, using basic skills they have acquired. This approach enables learners to make choices and is more effective than teacher-directed practical tasks.

> [W]here practical work is simply directed by the teacher, without learners making their own contribution to the planning, learning is less effective and learners show less evidence of developing both their skills and knowledge. Enquiry work can lead to high levels of motivation and engagement. (HMI, 2006)

Illustrative work is important as it enables learners to learn about science in a practical way by focusing upon a limited number of skills at any one time. These activities enable learners to concentrate upon the outcomes, as the 'what to do' and the 'how to do it' are prescribed by the teacher. Due to the formal nature of the illustration it is easy to focus learners' attention directly upon what is required. The methods of communication and recording can also be prescribed in illustrative work, and the activities undertaken provide experiences upon which future investigations can be based. Illustrative work provides opportunities for learners to experience aspects of scientific enquiry.

It is a myth that learners will become investigative scientists by a process similar to osmosis, picking up skills, attitudes and concepts by 'being there'!

Learners generate ideas and questions, but enabling them to answer these questions in a scientific way requires procedural understanding to be developed throughout the primary age range. The process should be started in the early years and the degree of challenge and the complexity of tasks increased as learners progress through the school. In order for the process to be successful there needs to be a common approach across the school, with all adults working in similar ways. This is known as continuity, and without a continuous approach it is unlikely that learners' learning will progress. In order to make this easier to manage there needs to be agreement about progression in procedural understanding which will result in all teachers knowing what learners have already been taught and where they are expected to progress to next. This is easier to achieve if the expectation for ways of working in all aspects of science is clearly stated for each year group. From a simple starting point in early years, learners will develop more independence. The level descriptions (Attainment Target 1) make it clear where progress should be focused at each level through the key stages. Using this information together with extensive opportunities to work with learners in whole-class investigative activities and in real settings allowed a suggested framework for progression to be constructed. Figures 5.2 (a) and (b) provide an opportunity for teachers to gain an understanding of where the age range they teach fits within the whole schemata and is a starting point for future discussion in schools.

The theory supporting this framework has as the central tenet that learners will make gains in understanding and skills, if development is in small steps and there is support from teachers and others. For learners to be successful, teachers have continually to aim to extend unaided achievement, by planning small steps and increasing the challenge. This is only effective when all teachers work to the same goals and realistic but challenging expectations are set from the start. It also requires a belief in the importance of procedural understanding.

Methods of Working

Young learners have their own ideas and are keen to find out about the world. When learners start school the whole process of investigation should begin, with the teacher supporting the work at all stages. A suitable idea can be generated from work already occurring in the classroom. Sometimes this can result from a suggestion made by a learner or it might be teacher directed: the teacher then models the investigative approach with the same variable being investigated by all the learners. By the age of 7, learners should have experience of a number of investigations. They will be used to working in groups and being supported by the teacher and their peers. They will be used to identifying variables from a global question and will be able to think of a question their group can answer. The learners will begin to take a more independent role and build upon the skills and experiences gained earlier in the key stage. The teachers/adults have an important role here in facilitating the work but not controlling it. By the time the learners are 9 years old the process should be further developed, with teachers supporting not directing. It is found to be

Key Stage 1

Aspects	Reception	Year 1	Year 2
Methods of working	Work is totally supported by adult	Beginning to work in groups supported by adults	Groups working on own investigations supported by planning format and class teachers
Question formation	Adult generates questions	Adult sets question. Pupils begin to raise own questions	Questions and suggestions made by pupils and they respond to teacher questions
Prediction	Pupils formulate idea/guess in head. Pupils are not asked what will happen?	Pupils are asked as a result of their work whether what happened was what was expected	Pupils are asked if what happened was expected and to give some reasons
Variables	Teacher selects variables e.g. type of material, amount of water	Teacher and pupils select variables e.g. type of material, amount of water, type of liquid	Teacher and pupils brainstorm variables then pupils choose e.g. types of material, amount of water, type of liquid, amount of material
Range and Interval	Range selected by teacher	Simple range discussed by pupils and teachers. Interval set by teacher	Range developed by the pupils e.g. three materials chosen. Interval discussed where relevant i.e. 0ml water, 50ml water, 100ml water
Choosing and Using Equipment	Everyday objects used, provided by teacher. Used with some support	Some everyday objects and simple equipment, sand timers, straws (non-standard measure) selected with limited support	Independent usage of simple equipment provided by teacher e.g. metre sticks, scales, tape measure
Observations and Measurements	Simple observations made e.g. wet/dry	Beginning to use non-standard measurements and to talk about their observations	Some use of standard units to measure length, mass. More than one reading beginning to be made. Observations used to make comparisons

Aspects	Reception	Year 1	Year 2
Oral Communication	Pupils respond to questions about their work. They are able to talk in sentences relating two events together	Pupils begin to talk about whether what happened was what they expected	Pupils make comparisons this cloth was more absorbent than that one. Some simple reasons are given
Written Communication	No written feedback expected. Emergent writing or Q and A by adult represents work	Simple writing to convey meaning used to communicate findings e.g. a letter to Alex's mum	Writing used to describe what happened. Scientific knowledge and understanding is developed through conclusion
Graphical Representation	Charts modelled by teacher begun to be drawn by pupils	Tables (2 columns) and charts produced by pupils with limited support. Bar charts are modelled by adult	Tables with space for a repeat reading introduced. Pupils draw bar charts. Adult helps with scale if appropriate. Patterns and trends are discussed as a class
Scientific Vocabulary	Simple words. Adult models correct vocabulary e.g. hard, soft, smooth	Vocabulary extended. Adults are still modelling. Displays provide important reinforcement	Pupils use simple vocabulary to explain results. Adult modelling and displays still very important. Concept maps/KWHL grids develop vocabulary
Health & Safety	Follows simple instructions when carrying out activities	Follows instructions when using equipment. Can respond to adult questions about safe working	Know about safe and careful working. Following instructions. Emphasis still on teacher to control hazards and risks

Figure 5.2a Progression of procedural understanding

Key Stage 2

Aspects	Year 3	Year 4	Year 5	Year 6
Methods of Working	Individual work within a group with some supported by adult	Teacher supports occasionally when needed. Pupils work in groups	Group working mainly unsupported.	No support for groups in normal situations. Scaffolds removed
Question Formation	After class brainstorms of global question, pupils start to raise own questions	Questions selected by pupils. Global question starts process	Opportunities are given for pupil questions to be followed as a result of an initial investigation	A range of questions is tested as a result of own ideas that arise from work. Not just of fair test variety
Prediction	Predictions are made with encouragement. Predictions include a reason	Level 3 predictions beginning to include knowledge and understanding	Predictions draw on past experience. Simple knowledge and understanding is used	Predictions are developed and explanations of these use sound understanding of area covered
Variables	Pupils with support, identify a range of variables that could be tested e.g. height, weight, material, size, way it is dropped, length of wing. Standard units are introduced	Pupils identify variables with limited support e.g. amount of soil, type of soil, amount of water, temperature of water	Scaffold used independently and a wide range of variables are identified e.g. type of substance, amount of liquid, size of container, amount of sugar, temperature of water, type of liquid, stir or not	Variables are identified by pupils and are chosen and manipulated ensuring a fair test if appropriate
Range and Interval	Pupils begin to understand the need range. Range chosen suits investigations e.g. 3 helicopters. Interval developed with help of teacher but is still non-standard e.g. small, medium and large	Range understood. Numbers used varies according to context but a minimum of 4 e.g. 4 types of soil, materials. Interval identified by pupils but still non-standard e.g. coarse, fine, thin materials	Range used independently and 5 or more are used routinely. The interval contains standard measurements and is systematically selected with some limited support from peers and teacher	Pupils use appropriate range to enable patterns and trends to be identified (6 as minimum). Pupils use K & U to identify appropriate intervals in a systematic way. Standard units are selected
Choosing and Using Equipment	Using simple equipment with some support e.g. thermometer, Newton meter, stop watch	Using equipment confidently with limited support to nearest whole number	Know what equipment to use selecting it themselves. Careful and correct usage to 1N, 1gm, 1mm, 1cm^3	Self-selecting using past experience. Range of equipment selected for a range of tasks. Repeated measurements taken which are precise

Aspects	Year 3	Year 4	Year 5	Year 6
Observations and Measurements	Simple observations used and measurements (3) accompany these. S.I. units of measurement for T°C, time, force	Three or more measurements taken routinely. S.I. units used with care. Scanning for unusual readings introduced	Dependent on context multiple readings become part of procedure. Unusual readings are discussed and repeated if time allows	Multiple measurements taken (6+). These are accurate. Unusual results are repeated automatically
Oral Communication	Teachers use feedback session to develop oral skills. Events described in order	Pupils report back with limited support. Teacher questioning used to develop explanations.	Teacher's role is to prompt when descriptions not explanations are given. Teachers and pupils ask questions to develop K and U. Systematic concise style encouraged.	Pupils report back including all relevant details. Explain what they found out and how they could improve their investigations. Teacher's role is as audience
Written Communication	Teacher models appropriate responses. Simple writing frame supports simple conclusions. Patterns and trends are written about. What did it mean? is more important than what I did	Explanations encouraged through written work. Patterns and trends developed. Questions Did the evidence support the prediction?, What do I know now that was not known before?	Method, apparatus conclusions are NOT recommended. Explanations are given, patterns and trends are discussed. Generalisations are included. Scaffolding is reduced	Scaffolding is reduced/removed. Conclusions draw on scientific K and U, the predictions and the evidence
Graphical Representation	Tables - 3 measurements and * (star) column are drawn unaided. Total or median is used. Bar charts produced unaided. Teacher helps pupils to identify the patterns and trends	Tables constructed unaided. Pupils check for unusual results with adults. Median used. Bar graphs constructed unaided. Patterns and trends discussed with limited support	Tables are sophisticated. Averages used. Unusual results discussed. Line graphs are drawn which have a few points and whole number scales. Decision about line/bar graph or scatter graph made in consultation with teacher	Tables are clearly presented. Average used where appropriate. Consolidation of line graphs, bar charts and scatter graphs. These have more points and complex scales. IT is used effectively. These graphical representations are used to draw results. Scientific vocabulary
Scientific Vocabulary	Vocabulary used to develop concepts. Correct vocabulary used to explain observations. Comparisons used effectively. KWHL grids/concept maps start process off	Correct vocabulary e.g. dissolving, melting, evaporating is used by teacher in course of work. Differences between the definitions of scientific words developed. Scientific vocabulary used as matter of course	Simple generalisation explained using correct vocabulary. Definitions of words used given by pupils e.g. gravity. Questioned by adults/peers. KWHL grids/concept maps still used as starting point	Scientific vocabulary used effectively to develop generalisations. KWHL grids/concept maps compared by pupils and definitions for words explained. Terms used effectively e.g. melting, dissolving, evaporating, condensing and in a range of contexts
Health & Safety	Knows term hazard and risk. Begins to use terms while assessing 'dangers' in practical work	Develops idea of recognising hazards and risks in investigative work. Can respond to questions	Begin to assess hazards and risks in their own work without prompts. Beginning to take action to control risks	Controls hazards and risks. Demonstrates in their work that they understand concept of hazard and risk

Figure 5.2b Progression of procedural understanding

most effective if direct adult support is reduced over time, with the reduction corresponding to the development of the learners' skills and abilities. Thus the role of the teacher is to model and support the learning processes throughout.

Whatever type of investigation is planned the teacher must identify in advance:

- what type of investigation will be undertaken
- the variables possible
- proposals for how and what data collection methods might be used.

As already stated in Chapter 2, trying to 'shoehorn' a fair test into a survey will result in strange results and confuse teachers and learners.

Question Formulation

In order to begin to investigate, an idea or a question is needed to stimulate thinking. With younger learners this process is new and, therefore, modelling and scaffolding at all stages is essential. Selecting a simple global question that results in few variables, where there are clear outcomes (results) and the context is related to real life, is central to success at this age. In Early Years classrooms, because adults provide the global questions and identify the variables to test, the focus is on providing opportunities to introduce the learners to the processes involved in testing out ideas. By the age of 7, learners will be able to respond to the global question and begin to identify variables themselves. The teacher will at this stage still be supporting the process. However, by the age of 11, learners should be able to think of their own questions as a result of ideas developed from illustrative tasks.

Setting the Context

In the initial stages it is necessary to introduce the learners to the problem they will have to help solve. This setting of the context is vital if the learners are to see the activity as having value. A range of new resources has been developing to target this area. The new resources all have a common feature: to present the problem or global question in a circumstance that the children understand. Many teachers use interactive whiteboards to deliver the story start in an appealing visual way. Caution should be used if this is the only type of science on offer to the learners as again the focus is on activities that have a fair test format. It also could become unappealing if used for seven years throughout the primary school, for although the learners are introduced to key characters in order to build familiarity, variety is said to be the spice of life! In some ways these latest innovations, using whiteboards to deliver information with notepads for recording and printable resource sheets, are still promoting a formulaic approach to primary science. However the activities are in clear, investigative settings. Other innovations include the use of puppets who present the problem to the learners and ask for their help (Keogh, Naylor, Downing, Maloney and Simon: 2005).

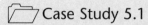

Case Study 5.1

A creative science subject leader decided to provide a context for some linked activities to develop scientific enquiry skills. The context given was that the school's competition cup had been stolen from the trophy cabinet. There were clues provided and four main suspects were identified. These were the headteacher, the science subject leader, a non-teaching assistant and the school's cook. Clues were provided near the scene of the crime and these had to be used to solve the crime. Learners compared fingerprints, shoe prints, hair samples, identified white powders and used chromatography on a pen left near the scene. Motivation was high and the teacher's role was to offer guidance and support, to organise mini-plenaries, to provoke thinking with questioning and to ensure that evidence was respected. The activity took three weeks of science lessons to complete and the learners wrote up their results as a newspaper article for the school newsletter. This approach ensures children use an ideas and evidence approach.

Planning investigations

If a fair test activity is selected, then the use of a planning format can support both teachers and learners. This modelling is necessary because it makes explicit that which is implicit in the process of investigating an idea. A range of types of scaffolds should be used, which increase in complexity throughout the primary years and many are based upon an original idea by Goldsworthy (1997). The Secondary science strategy has noted the values of this approach and examples can be downloaded and adapted from the web. http://www.bristol-cyps.org.uk/teaching/secondary/science/word/se_posters. doc

Pictorial clues, pictures of objects to change or measure rather than only written words, should be used with young learners wherever possible as a way of communicating effectively.

With experience the learners can identify a range of variables. Figure 5.3 demonstrates variables identified by a class of Year 2 learners investigating the global question 'Which tea bag makes the darkest dye?' The learners were introduced to different types of tea bags. They had not taken part in a complete investigation prior to this lesson, but were able to brainstorm all the factors in less than five minutes. They had, however, been introduced to an illustrative activity with one type of material, and three different tea bags, so they had some experience to draw upon. Although this activity was of a fair

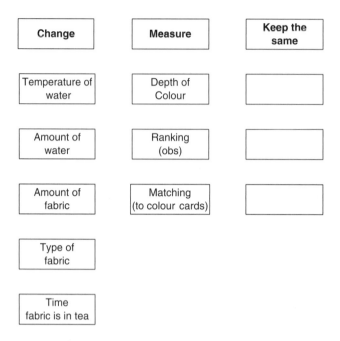

Figure 5.3 A Planning format , learners select 1 variable to change and then keep the rest the same.

test type, learners should also be introduced from an early age to sorting and classifying, surveying, problem solving and investigating change over time.

Case Study: 5.2

A group of Year 1 learners were investigating which of their torches was the brightest. They were provided with a range of torches, some plastic cups of different colours and samples of different materials. They were asked to think about how to find out which was the brightest torch. Their responses were recorded as a floor book (as discussed in Chapter 11), where everything they said was recorded in writing so that they could look at it later. When asked how they could find out which was the brightest torch,

Boy A said, 'The biggest one will be best, the blue one.'

Girl A said, 'Shine it on the floor and see which one shows up.'

Boy B said, 'Shine it on the board and see which one you can see.'

Learners were put into groups of 3s and were encouraged to think about how they would find out which was the brightest torch. They talked and then their ideas were shared. They began to see which torch shone through one cup, and then two and then three, etc. Some children saw the size of the light beam. They recorded their work by drawing around the torches and ranking them, using a star system, with ***** being very bright and* being not very bright. The lesson finished with children sharing their findings, which were recorded in words and pictures. The children's work and their thoughts were then made into a book for the learners to look at again and again. It was an investigation because each of the groups selected what they wanted to change and measure, they worked independently and were able to talk about what their group had found out. Although for this activity all groups worked at the same time it would have been just as effective for groups to work at different times throughout the week.

Problem Solving

Very effective enquiry can result from a problem or a challenge. Whilst electricity is a good context for this work, problem-solving activities are also effective within all areas of the science curriculum. The teacher could set a problem, such as, 'How can you protect the doll's house from burglars who are clever and might manage to beat a simple system?' or 'Can you make a lighthouse that will keep ships safe?' or, 'How can you make the fairy on top of the Christmas tree light up?' In these types of activities it is not suitable to use a fair test and the scientific enquiry skills used by the learners will be enhanced and not reduced because of this. One teacher undertook a problem-solving approach when working with living things in the environment. She told her class that they had to decide where the most appropriate place would be for a new playground. The learners set off to survey the school grounds, ensuring the place chosen would have as little impact on the living things found in different parts of the school grounds as possible. Plans, maps and posters were created to show where most living things were found and to suggest the most environmentally appropriate place for the site of the new play equipment.

Whether the activity is a fair test, a survey, watching change over time or a problem-solving task, talking about what could be done and deciding on things that can be changed and measured will support learners in the initial stages of investigating. This is particularly true when their experience of working on tasks by themselves is limited. Learners will need to be supported through the process, as having choice is so unusual for some learners that they take some time to realise they need to think for themselves.

Case Study: 5.3

The learners in this case study were aged between 9 and 10 and their normal science lessons started with a PowerPoint that told them the subject knowledge that they needed to know, included some demonstrations

(Continued)

(Continued)

that one or two learners took part in and concluded with a 'write up' of what they had seen and listened to. It was decided that they needed to be more motivated towards science and to take a more active role in their learning. So the questions were posed, 'Why do seeds bother with dispersal?' and 'How many different ways are there?' The lesson started with boxes of fruits and seeds being handed to the groups for them to observe and sort. The boxes contained horse chestnuts, strawberries, sweet chestnuts in their cases, acorns, burrs, Sticky Willie (also known as catch weed, *Galium aparine*), mangetout, sugar snap peas, a small orange, blackberries, a poppy head, honesty seeds. The learners discussed in groups what they thought the seeds would do, although their first question was could they open the peas? They then sorted the fruits into different groups and explained their grouping. Questions were posed as to how the seeds would move away from the parent plant and whether there were clues that could be found. The learners recorded their work as a series of annotated diagrams and grouped all the similar seeds together. Strawberries caused some problems, as the seeds were not in the centre where the learners thought they would be. They then sorted and grouped the seeds and discussed the ways they were dispersed. The teacher than asked the learners to role play how one seed was dispersed from the parent plant giving reasons why it should do so. This enabled some on-the-spot assessment to occur. Learners demonstrated their understanding of what seeds need in order to grow, by explaining through the drama how it could be dark and dry nearer to the parent plant and the competition would not be good for the young seedlings. The lesson then moved on to asking the learners to create their own special seed. They had to decide what it was like, where it would live, how it would be dispersed and what method would be appropriate. At the end of the lesson, most learners stated they had had fun, the quality of their ideas demonstrated learning and they were beginning to think for themselves. This lesson was investigative as the learners had to make choices about how to group and compare seeds, using evidence to support their ideas. They also had to make choices about their imaginary seed which used their subject knowledge.

Group work

Learners should work in small group situations from the Early Years onwards. However, in the Early Years the activity is likely to be tackled by the learners individually taking turns, rather than as a co-operative working group. What is important is the opportunity for learners to be introduced to practices, which will be refined throughout their education. There is no requirement that all groups should work at the same time, and the investigation could be a

Figure 5.4   Learners adopting roles within an investigation. Equipment Manager (experimenter), Recording Manager (Communicator) and Measurement Manager (Observer)

teacher-directed small group task, if this suits the learning needs of the learners or overall plans. Although many learners sit in groups, few groups actually work together; in science, investigative activities enable groups' working skills to be developed. However, the size and composition of the group is important for effective working. If the groups are too large then each learner will not have enough to do, resulting in time to be 'off task'. If all the learners are of a similar ability they might not want to listen to each other or may lack the skills to speak and listen with confidence. If the groups are too large then it will be more problematic to reach an agreement about the task to be undertaken. Groups of three seem to be most effective for whole investigations where learners are planning and carrying out their own ideas. It can be effective to give these learners labels to help them with their group work skills. One can be the 'observer' whose role is to record or watch what happens. Another can be the 'communicator' whose role is to record the results and be ready to report back to the class. The final role is the 'experimenter', the learner who will undertake the task, Figure 5.4. In most investigations these roles can be changed so that each learner undertakes each role, and the activity is replicated three times, which will enhance the reliability of the work. On some occasions it is just as effective to change the roles in the group for each lesson. Later in the key stage, for time management and learning reasons, it is more effective for all learners to work at the same time. By the age of 11, most learners can work effectively in groups and the class shares conclusions at the end of the session.

⌐ Case Study 5.4

Always starting an investigation with a question may not enable learners to develop all their scientific skills. Often lessons are not long enough for a whole investigation and as a result more directed work can occur. This often results in limited opportunities for children to take ownership of their learning and to work co-operatively. Providing learners with a number of open-ended challenges is one way of starting investigative science activities and putting the learners in control of their learning, within carefully decided boundaries.

Figure 5.5   Living things box

Learners were provided with a letter from an alien who wanted to know about their planet and what they understood about various scientific topics. Within the letter the alien posed questions that covered the main misconceptions that primary children hold on the area under study (SPACE, 1998). The letter was accompanied by a decorated box of science equipment, which the learners could use to answer the questions posed by the alien (Figure 5.5). Included with the box was a range of everyday materials and some specialised science equipment. Learners had to decide what the equipment was for and how they could use it to answer the questions posed within the letter. Initially they undertook a period of exploration, then started to suggest simple experiments, investigations and problem-solving activities. They reported their work back to the alien as a series of postcards, posters or PowerPoint productions which each answered the alien's questions. In total

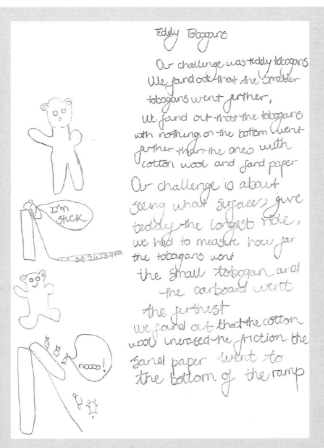

Figure 5.6 Two children's response to a forces challenge

10 boxes were used with learners in a number of schools across one local author-ity. (Figure 5.6, Feedback from forces box). The advantage of this approach was that it provided challenges for the learners and ensured they had to think for themselves. There was no right answer to find and they did not need to prove anything. The need to find out the answers to the questions posed by the letter ensured the work stayed within the requirements of the National Curriculum and an added advantage was that, by explaining to an alien, the learners were explaining and using scientific vocabulary continually.

While it is important to provide interesting and open-ended contexts, learners also need to be supported with some basic skills such as tables and graphs.

Tables, Charts and Graphs

Even the youngest learners are capable of creating a simple chart with help. Drawing the chart is a skill and thus can be modelled to the whole class, and then additional support can be provided for those learners who have difficulty

Chart

Change	Observe
☐	✓
▮	×
▭	×

Real objects. Standard measurements, median and mode used

Simple 2 C table

Change	Observe/Measure
☐	3
▮	3
▭	1

Pictorial representation of objects. Non-standard measurement and ranking

4 C table

Change	Measure	*
☐		
▮		
▭		

Pictorial and written objects. Standard measurements, adding totals

5 C table

Change	Measure	*
Brown		
Caster		
Granul-ated		
Coffee		

Written objects. Standard measurements, median and mode used

6 C table

Change	Measure	*
10cm		
12cm		
14cm		
16cm		
18cm		

Standard measurements, median, mode used. Identification of unusual results expected

7 C table

Change	Obser-vations	Measure	*
10			
20			
30			
40			
50			
60			
70			

Range of results over time, with accuracy of readings. Selection of all responsibility of pupils. Use of mean, mode or median

Figure 5.7 Table development scaffolds

with this form of representation; interestingly, such learners often have diffi-culties later with drawing graphs. At these early stages it is important that the charts are very simple and directly related to the activity. For example, if the activity is to find a material suitable for an umbrella, a sample of each of the materials to be tested can be stuck into the chart, because drawings and other representations are too difficult for many learners at this stage.

While it is important for the adults to understand the progression of the skills of enquiry, this can also be communicated to the learners by changing the scaf-folds that are in use. An example is provided for constructing tables (Figure 5.7). This shows progression from simple charts to two-column tables (2 C tables) and eventually to tables that can include a range of measurements and observations.

There is no expectation that young learners will construct their own graphs. It is important to note that time spent with young learners constructing pic-tograms can sometimes contribute to problems with graphs at a later stage, i.e. numbers drawn in the boxes, rather than on the lines. By 7 years learners should be able to draw their own simple bar graph with limited support relating to the selection of scale. By 11 years learners should be confident enough to draw line and scatter graphs. It is important that these skills are initially developed outside the framework of investigations. Many investigations falter at this point because without graphs, learners are unable to complete the process, as they cannot identify clear patterns and trends from which to draw conclusions.

Communicating Results and Concluding

When communicating findings, learners need to be provided with many oppor-tunities and styles. How the results are communicated should vary according to the age of the learners as well as the enquiry type, as discussed in Chapter 2. While young learners are developing their ability to use written language, an approach focused completely upon this mode will be unsuccessful. When the observational part of an activity is completed, the work should be discussed orally and the outcomes shared visually; making a wall display or putting some outcomes into a class 'scrap book' celebrates this work (see Chapter 11).

In complete investigations learners should be enabled to demonstrate their skills. Learners who find written responses difficult should be supported and provided with prompts to help their writing. Writing frames became *de rigueur* in many schools at the height of the literacy strategy. However, providing the same scaffold at the end of each investigation limits motivation and creativity.

Creativity occurs when time and choice are provided. This was demon-strated by a Year 1 child investigating the global question 'How to keep teddy dry'. She used all the materials she had tested to make a collage of the teddy, with the umbrella made of foil, the material that she had found to be water-proof. In addition, she had stuck a flap on her work, which when lifted had the word 'foil' written underneath. Her response took no longer than any other child's but was even more outstanding as this was the first lesson in the term where she completed a lesson in an appropriate manner.

Writing a letter to explain results is effective, especially if the letters are posted and responses are received. Survey investigations such as the washing-up liquid producing the most bubbles, the strongest kitchen towel, the most effective toothpaste or the strongest tea bags offer great opportunities for letter writing. Not all conclusions have to be written; pictures can convey meaning and adults can ask questions and scribe responses for future reference. News reports and role-play enable learners to demonstrate their understanding, which is the main point of concluding and explaining the results. Picture boards and story boards also make excellent communication strategies.

Limiting the level of attainment

Sometimes the activities set for learners will reduce their ability to demonstrate high levels of scientific skills. For example, when undertaking investigations on spinners, if the learners only change the type of material and keep everything else the same and measure the time taken in the air, then the end result will be lower than if they change the size of the spinner systematically and record the time in the air. Changing systematically the area or length of the wing requires more skill than just changing the materials, and the end results of changing the size would result in a line graph, whilst changing materials will only result in a bar chart. It is important when setting out investigative work that the teacher encourages his or her most able scientists to try out challenging activities.

▢ Summary

Procedural understanding involves all the processes used when investigating an idea. It represents the ways scientists work. These skills need to be taught to learners but learners also need to have opportunities to undertake the process of investigating an idea themselves, going through all the stages of scientific enquiry. A framework was presented to help with continuity and progression throughout the primary age range. As scientists tackle different questions in different ways, so learners need opportunities to carry out 'a fair test', surveys, sorting and comparisons, problem solving and to investigate changes over time.

Further Reading

Feasey, R. (2006) 'Scientific investigations in the context of enquiry', in Harlen, W. (ed.) *ASE Guide to Primary Science Education*. Hatfield: ASE.

Johnson, J. (2005) 'The importance of exploration', in Bruce, T. *Critical Issues in Early Childhood Education*. Maidenhead: Open University Press.

Keogh, B., Naylor, S., Downing, B., Maloney, J. and Simon, S. (2006) 'Puppets bringing stories to life in science', *Primary Science Review* 92, 26–8.

Newton, D.P. (2002) *Talking Sense in Science: Helping Children Understand Through Talk*. London and New York: Falmer.

6

Planning and Assessing Learning

Hellen Ward

Introduction

Assessment is a combination of all the processes used to plan and evaluate lessons appropriately in order to facilitate optimum learning and to ensure that learners achieve to the best of their ability. Assessment is much more than merely recording and reporting. This chapter will explore the whole area of assessing science in the primary classroom.

Assessing Learners' Learning in Science

There are only three ways of gaining evidence about how learners are learning:

- by observation
- through discussion
- by marking/looking at completed tasks.

Teachers often hold unrealistic expectations of their own assessment of learners, which often affect their assessments in science: it is not possible to listen to every conversation or to observe every learner in every situation, and a focus solely on the completed task can be very limiting. Carefully considered choices have to be made about what assessment information is to be collected, how it is to be collected and how it will be used. Involving other adults is helpful but involving learners is essential.

In science, observation of learners is vital. Through observing them working, judgements can be made about their ability to use equipment, the way they carry out an investigation and their co-operation with others, as well as about their attitudes in learning, such as creativity and perseverance. By observing how a learner undertakes tasks, information about current and future learning needs can identified.

Discussions with learners and 'listening in' to those between learners are essential as these provide information about individual and collective ideas and thought processes. These also provide important insights into the ways of working and other information about the concepts and processes the learners are using. Realistically, since it is impossible to be present at all significant moments in every learner's work in science, a schedule should be constructed for observing, and speaking with, all learners over time: focused observations. This should not, however, deter adults from recording 'significant' points of note for individual pupils, whenever they happen.

In reality it is mainly completed tasks that teachers assess through marking: the written outcomes, the drawings and diagrams, or responses to practice test questions. These, though, will not provide the 'full 'picture' of the processes and learning that have taken place. It is therefore important to use a mix of all three approaches, but also to understand that each has advantages and disadvantages. For example, with older learners, assessing completed tasks can provide reasonable information, whilst with younger learners, those for whom English is an additional language or those with special educational needs, the assessment of written tasks will provide limited insight, particularly about processes of learning.

Assessment for Learning

The Assessment Reform Group (ARG, 1999) defined the terms 'assessment for learning' and 'assessment of learning'. Assessment for learning is the formative processes used to develop learners' learning; the knowledge of where learners are at a given time and the skills of enabling them to progress to where they need to be. Assessment of learning is often considered as a national, or end of unit, test but it can be any method that judges learning at a given time.

The purposes of assessment include the following:

- the promotion of effective learning for each learner
- the regular reporting on the learning of individual learners to interested parties (parents, carers and other teachers)
- the awarding and accrediting of learning (examinations and qualifications)
- the monitoring standards of schools and teaching (league tables and OfSTED)
- the monitoring of standards at regional and national level (political and international comparisons) (adapted from Harlen, 2007).

The introduction of national testing in England and the annual publication of school results has led to judgements that link quality of teaching to test outcomes. As always when such links are made, teachers adapt their approach, a phenomenon observed in many countries. This then impacts on the way learners are taught (Assessment Reform Group (ARG), 2006). A direct outcome can be that areas not tested become 'less important' with a corresponding emphasis on teaching strategies to 'pass the test'. 'Teaching to the test' practice often begins in Year 5, if not before, and in some schools happens throughout Key Stage 2. The focus on the assessment of learning in this way can have a negative impact upon teaching, although science's status as a core subject in the national curriculum is as a direct result of its assessment by national tests.

Planning science learning starts with the long-term plan. Each school has its own ethos and identity, indeed this is encouraged through *Excellence and Enjoyment* (DfES, 2003). The long-term plan maps the appropriate experiences the school provides for learners to gain the knowledge and understanding and to acquire the skills outlined in the national statutory documents from the Foundation Stage to the end of Key Stage 2. The plan should indicate the time allowed for each subject but also make clear where links between subjects provide for more realistic experiences in learning. National schemes do not reflect local or individual school contexts and, as a result, many schools, particularly at Key Stage 1, are beginning to plan science that matches their needs (Ofsted/HMI, 2004). This is a positive move. Another positive move is the suggestion that all learners should have learning that is personalised.

> Personalised learning demands teaching and learning strategies that develop the competence and confidence of every learner by actively engaging and stretching them (DfES, 2007).

> In order to personalise learning, teachers need to assess their learners. They need to know about where learners currently are, where they need to get to and also how they will bridge the gap between the two. (Wiliam, 2003).

Personalised learning means taking an approach that responds to each learner's needs by:

- strengthening the link between learning and teaching
- engaging the learners as partners in learning: connecting learning to what they already know and can do
- encouraging learners to be active and curious
- encouraging them to create their own hypotheses and ask their own questions
- helping learners to set their own goals
- encouraging learners to take risks while taking account of health and safety issues
- involving learners in self-and peer-assessment.

Many readers will identify that personalised learning in science has the same philosophy and aims as assessment for learning.

Planning for Assessment

Medium-term plans provide details of specific learning objectives, the opportunities for meeting them, the resources required and assessment strategies to be used. In some schools the QCA/DfEE (1998) scheme of work or a similar published document will be used. Although not statutory, such a scheme reduces the need for teachers to make decisions about time and content to ensure the needs of learners are met. Effective medium-term planning provides the structure for the personalising of learning at the classroom level.

Science is about knowledge and understanding, but it is also about progression in acquiring skills and developing procedures. A medium-term plan should outline progression in all areas of science in a primary school from Year R through to Year 6. Using the plan to track an 'imaginary' learner as they move through the school, it is possible to plot the science the learner would experience and to identify both the areas of learning that occur regularly and those aspects not covered so often. Through work with science co-ordinators, it is apparent that many learners are exposed to a great deal of repetition. Using 'food and healthy eating' as an example, lack of progress occurs when 'a healthy meal' is repeatedly the focus for learning. Although science teaching is cyclical and aspects should be revisited, learning must be developed and this is unlikely to be achieved by revisiting the same activity again and again.

This lack of progression is found with many other units. Problems occur when repeated experiences have no development, while clear planning ensures learners' experiences and opportunities are developed and motivation is encouraged. National schemes may help with planning for progression, however they need to be reviewed critically. It is important that each school tailors the scheme to the needs of their learners. Just because a published scheme has the 'seal of an expert', a pushy salesperson, or an attractive, glossy presentation does not mean it is perfect for every school. Many reception classes teach units on what plants need in order to grow and parts of the plant and this work is then repeated in Year 1 – often using a limited range of plants.

In the QCA/DfEE (1998) science scheme, sound is covered in Year 1 and not again until Year 5. However, the learners' answers given in national tests and discussed in the annual standards report (e.g. QCA/NAA, 2006), indicate that learners' understanding of sound is not well developed. In part, this underdevelopment of aspects of sound might be linked to an overall lack of music teaching. The Office for Standards in Education and HMI (2004) acknowledge that a curriculum that focuses mainly upon numeracy and literacy will affect other areas of learning. This illustrates why schools need to identify appropriate links in the curriculum that enrich learning and meet the needs of their learners. Breadth and balance are also important, but in the QCA/DfEE scheme there are many more units that focus on Life and Living Processes (Sc2) compared to units on Materials and their Properties (Sc3), or Physical Processes (Sc4).

After tracking learning across the school, it is important to look at what learners receive in each year. This is not only the responsibility of a science subject leader but also of the class teacher. This level of scrutiny should focus upon the experience and opportunities for science. It is at this level that learning can be personalised. If science is only perceived as a body of knowledge, then the focus will merely be on subject knowledge learning intentions, so revision might be necessary to ensure the development of skills is optimised.

The way lessons build upon each other also needs ongoing evaluation and the time provided for learners to develop their ideas and skills needs consideration. One reason learners give for not liking science is that they are not aware of links and progression in learning. 'Every lesson is different and there is no link to what we have done before', said a less literate boy in Year 5. The amount of unfinished work seen in many exercise books supports this 'stretch it thin' approach.

The development of skills (see Chapter 2) is an area gaining importance in science teaching, but if learning is going to be successful for all learners, then understanding of, and working with, the National Curriculum level descriptions are essential. The learning and attainment of each cohort of learners will vary but so will each learner's progress in each aspect of science. These differences are not just in understanding but also include experiences, expectations and enjoyment. Although the national expectation in England for most learners in Year 2 is Level 2 and in Year 6 is Level 4, this is a broad-brush approach and teachers need to know what skills, processes and understanding are required to meet each level, and to plan with these in mind. By sharing an understanding of the elements of the level descriptions, in words they can understand, learners can begin to recognise where they are and what they need to do to improve their learning. This is vital if the learning is to be personalised and for assessment for learning to occur.

Teaching and learning are often discussed together as though inextricably linked; however, just because teaching occurs, learning is not guaranteed. Understanding the progression of skills enables the different needs of all the learners in a particular age group to be met. This differentiation is vital and needs to occur in every lesson.

 Case Study 6.1

In a Year 2 class studying materials and their properties, the expectation was initially set at Level 2, *Making a number of observations*. However, within the class there were learners who were not working at this level. The learning intention that was shared with the children remained the same: '*To observe how things change*', but the activity/outcome was altered slightly using success criteria:

- to draw one bag and use some words to show changes
- to compare more than one bag and use words to show how they have changed
- to be able to make some measurements and record these

This enabled learners working at Level 1 *to observe and communicate in simple ways*, whilst more able learners were able to make *more observations and some measurements*. Here, the majority of learners were working at Level 2, so were expected to make comparisons. With 30 learners in the class, basing all assessment of learning on observation or discussion only was impossible, so a mix of approaches was used. For most learners the outcome was demonstrated as a completed task, which was a set of drawings with some words; for other learners, information was obtained through discussion.

(Continued)

(Continued)

There was little opportunity for direct observation but questioning by the teacher occurred. The more able learners were able to add measurements to their observations, while less able learners only drew one picture and were supported with writing by using sticky labels with words on. Planning totally different tasks for the range of abilities usually results in teachers supporting tasks and not teaching learners – the juggling the balls and plate-spinning type of lesson – here all the learners had the same basic activity. It was important to consider the challenge factor in this activity, as learners who are given low-level tasks and less interesting equipment can become bored and uninterested.

It will have struck some readers that the activity that the learners were undertaking was not focused upon. This omission relates to the issue of activity rather than learning-driven science lessons. The activity was a melting experience using the bags referred to in Chapter 9 (odd one out, Figure 9.5, placed in hand-hot water). If the activity had been selected first then learning could be reduced to knowing that some materials change, which makes it even more problematic to match the needs of each learner. In the example, however, it was the skills that were the focus and the change was the context. The learners do remember that materials change but are also encouraged to practise their skills, thus providing more clear opportunities for differentiated learning.

Assessment for Learning in Science

Assessment for learning has received a great deal of publicity, from the publishing of *Inside the Black Box* (Black and Wiliam, 1998) to current research projects in many schools both in the UK and beyond. It is not a set of procedures but an opportunity to place the learners in the driving seat of learning. This need for learners to take control of their learning is where at times assessment for learning has not been successful. It is hard for some teachers to change long-held practices and to empower learners. Some teachers have thought that it was enough merely to carry out the strategies, such as sharing learning intention, peer assessment and feedback marking. Sutton (2007) termed this 'assessment for teaching' and suggests that without the learners taking control of their learning, there will be little noticeable change.

Assessment for learning in science requires learners to understand what they already know and be aware of what they still need to know. So the first stage in planning should include some ways of activating the learners' prior knowledge. Regardless of age, learners are not blank canvases or vessels to be filled. They have ideas and understanding about the world and it would be counterproductive to ignore this. A starting point could be KWHL grids (as discussed in Chapter 2) or mind maps (Figure 6.1). A personalised learning project funded by AstraZeneca Science Teaching Trust with 30 teachers provided the example below.

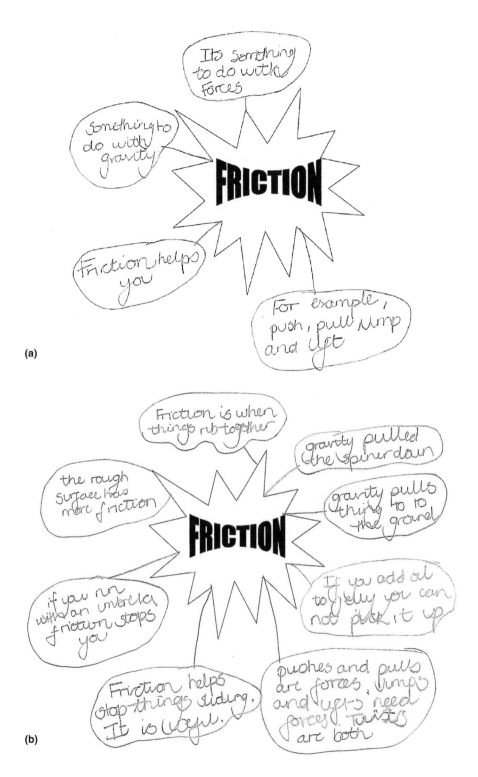

Figure 6.1   Before and after, mind maps: what I know about friction (Yr 4)

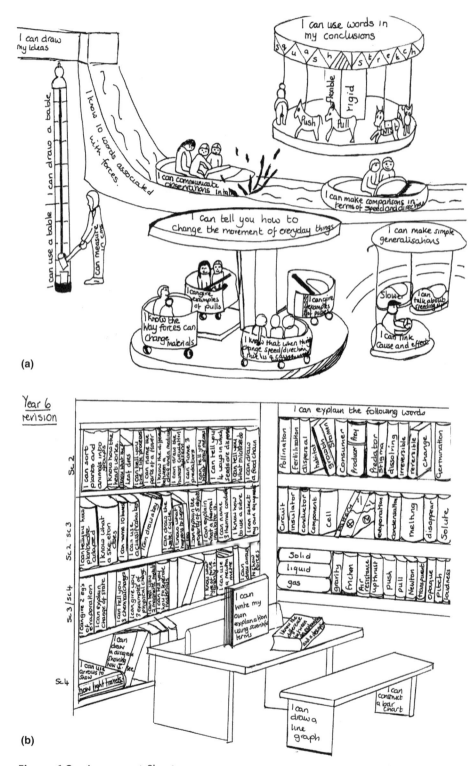

Figure 6.2   Assessment Sheets

These were from a Year 4 class who were studying friction. At the start of the topic they had little knowledge and understanding and poor attitudes to science. By the end of the topic a greater understanding was obtained. One of the main learning points for some was that they enjoyed the activity.

When the ideas that the learners hold and the vocabulary currently in use are identified, it is then possible to help learners to understand what they will need to know by the end of the topic. This could be by using pictorial assessment sheets. An example of this is provided in Figure 6.2. With younger learners this could be undertaken by the children and the teachers together, while older learners can take more responsibility and be instrumental in monitoring their own progress.

Using the assessment outcomes is also helpful when planning lessons. The National Curriculum level descriptions for knowledge and understanding can be used to identify progress level by level across the programme of study (DfES, 1999). Using Sc2, Sc3 and Sc4 only and starting with Level 1, key words can be identified. For example, across all three aspects Level 1 is about communicating observations in oral and written form. The understanding needed at Level 2 is about sorting, grouping and classifying. Incidentally, this comparison element of Level 2 is also in history and geography and allows further links between subjects. Level 3 can be classified as 'cause and effect', for example, overeating causes weight gain, rougher surfaces have greater friction. These simple generalisations are usually difficult for learners at Key Stage 1 to understand.

Figure 6.3 demonstrates the progression at each level. This can be used to plan learning intentions, using the idea that 'If I know what I am looking for, I am more likely to spot it when it happens'. When used in this way the lesson has an appropriate pitch and the focus is on learning rather than activity. It also enables learners to know what they are expected to be able to do. So learners working at Level 4 would know that their work must contain explanations and use scientific vocabulary.

Level	Knowledge expected
1	Communicate observations
2	Sort group, compare, similarities and differences
3	Cause and effect, simple generalisations and simple explanations
4	Explanations using scientific vocabulary. Generalisations
5	Abstract ideas and models

Figure 6.3 Knowledge at different levels

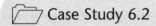 Case Study 6.2

The Year 2 learners were still undertaking work on materials and their properties. The activity related to rocks. The knowledge requirement for the learners was set according to Level 2, in line with national expectations. The learning intention shared with the learners was '*to sort objects into groups and to make a simple record*'.

The success criteria were:

- to be able groups rocks that share the same property
- to be able to record these groups
- to be able to use some words to explain grouping.

A few of the learners were not yet at the level where they could sort and group and draw pictures, so they were given hoops in which to put their rocks and some support through questioning and discussion. Another group were beginning to sort, so they were given a small number of samples with very obvious properties. They had previously been supported with small hoops and vocabulary cards. Most of the rest of the class were sorting and grouping and drawing the results in their books. They exchanged ideas and used their own science dictionaries for appropriate words. The higher-achieving learners explained their sorting using a greater number of rock samples, some of which required more than simple observation by sight.

In this lesson no additional support was provided, but if there had been, then the lower ability group could have been given opportunities to work with an adult, to extend their vocabulary, or one of the middle groups could have been questioned and challenged to give simple explanations for their groupings. Assessment was relatively easy because the learning intention and success criteria were clear and had been shared with learners in language they understood and the majority of the learning was pitched at Level 2. Towards the end of the session the learners evaluated their work, deciding if they had achieved the success criteria. Those that did drew a smiley face, if not then a sad face was drawn. The learners were clear about the purpose of this, and assessed themselves well. It had taken some weeks to familiarise them with this method. Some learners drew a straight mouth on their face, as they were unsure. At the end of the lesson the books were reviewed. Some learners were only able to draw the rocks but were also able to talk about them using science words provided by the teacher. They were not working at Level 2 and needed more support. Most learners were able to compare and sort (they had met the learning intention) and a few learners provided simple explanations. This demonstrated that they were working at a higher level. These assessments were fed directly into the next lesson.

Sharing Learning Intentions

Many teachers now plan lessons by identifying learning intentions. Often, however, there are too many learning intentions in a single lesson and this confuses both teacher and learner. Evidence demonstrates that sharing learning intentions is vital and that writing it on the board or displaying it in a prominent place is also important. These should be written in 'child speak', thus enabling learners to talk about what they are going to learn and to think about how they will know they have learnt this. If learning intentions are not shared in this way, then the link between the learning of the lesson and the learners' ability to self assess is lost. Writing the learning intention on the board in Reception classrooms enables learners to identify and talk about the learning in the lesson even though the learners cannot read the words themselves. It does, however, contribute to them learning to read. Where the learning intention was only shared orally in a Year 2 class, even the literate able learners were not sure what the lesson was about.

When planning learning, Clarke (2003) stresses the importance of separating the learning intention from the context of the learning. In Case Study 6.2 the learning intention is, 'to sort objects into groups', and it is important learners understand that they are learning to sort. The context in this case happens to be rocks, but it could be any other material. If this separation of intention and context is not clear, then, Clarke has found, the learners become more focused on the rocks than on sorting. In order to move learning forward it is important in planning to consider the following questions:

- What will this lesson look like when it is completed?
- Which learner/s need(s) to be extended further?
- Which learner or groups of learners will need to be supported?
- Will non-teaching assistants, teachers or learners provide the support?
- How will the learners communicate their findings?
- Will a worksheet provide the outcome required?

Worksheets have some benefits but often only when produced in-house to meet a specific purpose. However, many worksheets used to provide differentiation often contribute to lack of challenge and excitement in science lessons. Key issues teachers need to consider are the level of literacy of the materials, the type of words used and the density of text. Many commercially produced worksheets that can be photocopied promote science as a comprehension activity, a colouring sheet or 'flat work'. A 5-year-old learner at the start of Year 1 coined this term. When asked about his view of learning, he stated that it was better in Reception because in Year 1 it was all 'flat work'. On closer questioning it was revealed that in Reception opportunities were provided to build, explore and investigate, but in Year 1 this was replaced by endless sheets of paper, 'flat work'! The cost to science budgets for worksheets is enormous, with some schools spending so much on photocopies that they have inadequate science resources. The cost to learning is priceless.

Evidence of achievement has been one of the difficult issues over the last decade and has contributed to poor practice. The use of worksheets can de-skill learners, whilst encouraging learners to do their own drawings, take photographs and construct tables produces considerable learning gains with the acquisition of science skills, enjoyment by learners and a reduction in budget costs. When the same approach is introduced at Key Stage 2 the process is harder because learners have lost their independence and it takes time to regain this or learn the skills. Initially, books are untidy but the end results are worthwhile both for teachers and learners. Observations and discussions with learners using worksheets demonstrated that the focus was on completing the sheet rather than learning. When one learner is doing the work and the rest of the group are copying, assessment is difficult. It is impossible to assess understanding with work copied off the board. The enjoyment and creativity of learning should not be stifled by the chore of recording, and this mechanistic approach will not enable self-assessment or feedback marking.

Evaluating Learning

Grouping should be based on assessment of learners' scientific knowledge, understanding and skills, and not on ability in any other subject. Grouping in science needs to vary according to the aspect being taught, as attainment might vary across aspects. For example a 'less able' Year 1 child was able to lead the class session on electricity, as he knew what electricity was, where it came from and how it was created at a power station. This knowledge was as a result of out-of-school learning, and it helped that his father was an electrician! He was able to produce and understand electrical circuits, draw diagrams and communicate his understanding at a much higher level than the other learners. The class teacher encouraged and developed his skills and as a result his self-esteem was raised.

Whenever learning is assessed a judgement is also being made on the quality of the teaching. At the end of a lesson reflect upon:

- the elements that were successful
- the level of learner motivation
- the clarity of teacher explanations
- the effectiveness of resources
- the effectiveness of the activities.

These evaluations help to adjust the lesson next time this unit is taught as well as inform the next lesson in the series. It is important that the lessons in a unit are not set in concrete with the sole intention to get through them: learners' progress and learning are the first priority. At the end of a lesson it can be helpful to record and evaluate the learning.

Figure 6.4 provides an example of a simple formative system. Up arrows demonstrate attainment above the expected (a more challenging task now needs to be set!), dots mean that these learners achieved appropriately, and down arrows indicate learners that did not meet the intentions (and therefore need further support). The next lesson should be amended in light of this and a series of assessments will provide information on attainment and indicate changes in overall performance for a particular learner. For example, if a learner who had been achieving highly starts to perform less well, this should

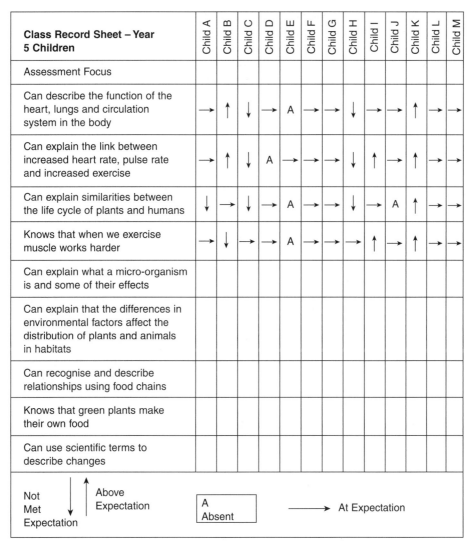

Class Record Sheet – Year 5 Children	Child A	Child B	Child C	Child D	Child E	Child F	Child G	Child H	Child I	Child J	Child K	Child L	Child M
Assessment Focus													
Can describe the function of the heart, lungs and circulation system in the body	→	↑	↓	→	A	→	→	↓	→	→	↑	→	→
Can explain the link between increased heart rate, pulse rate and increased exercise	→	↑	↓	A	→	→	→	↓	↑	→	↑	→	→
Can explain similarities between the life cycle of plants and humans	↓	→	↓	→	A	→	→	↓	→	A	↑	→	→
Knows that when we exercise muscle works harder	→	↓	→	→	A	→	→	→	↑	→	↑	→	→
Can explain what a micro-organism is and some of their effects													
Can explain that the differences in environmental factors affect the distribution of plants and animals in habitats													
Can recognise and describe relationships using food chains													
Knows that green plants make their own food													
Can use scientific terms to describe changes													

Not Met Expectation ↓   Above Expectation ↑   A Absent   → At Expectation

Figure 6.4 Simple formative system

be investigated. It could be the aspect of science that is a problem, or that they missed a lesson where a key skill was taught, or that there are issues at home. This type of assessment is only formative if it is acted upon by the teacher and/or learner (Black and Wiliam, 1998).

After each activity learners should know if they have met the learning intention and be given opportunities for future action. Feedback marking and feedforward planning needs to occur on a lesson-by-lesson basis until the very end of the unit of work, when a summative judgement is made. This should be recorded, as next half-term the work will be in a different aspect of science. The end-of-unit judgement will contribute to information about the learners' progress over the year and will be reported to parents and other colleagues. If level descriptions are used to plan the learning intentions then the level a learner is working at is known (Figure 6.4). Assessment for learning in science only works if learners and teachers take action on learning needs. If books are marked with a comment of 'good', there is no action to take the learning forward, as well as no indication about why it was good or if it was all good. In science, symbol marking works very effectively. The symbols used should be discussed with the learners.

Case Study 6.3

The school was a small village school and Ofsted inspectors had identified assessment in science as an issue. The learners in Class 4 were a mixed ability group of 28 boys and girls aged 10 and 11 years. The topic for the half-term was materials and their properties, and the teacher was keen to trial feedback marking. The learners chose smiley faces to be used where work was good and met the learning intention; this was unexpected because of their age but it was unanimous. It was also agreed that on any piece of work two smiley faces would be recorded. Providing three for some, two for others or only providing one would be the same as giving numbers out of 10 or grades, which is known to be de-motivational for all but the brightest learners. A triangle was chosen to indicate where the piece of work could be improved. At the end of each lesson work was marked and areas for improvement highlighted. The learners then used the first five minutes of the following science lesson to look at what had been judged as good and to act upon the area for improvement. This provided a clear link between lessons as well as a clear and calm start. Opportunities for the teacher to talk with individual learners to provide additional support were also possible. The learners liked the system and always acted upon the marking. There was a steady improvement in the work of learners of all abilities.

Interestingly, after four or five weeks one child's work began to deteriorate, and despite looking very thoroughly at a piece of work only one smiley face was given. At the beginning of the next lesson Darren complained he only had one smiley face. Darren was challenged to find, and justify, where another smiley face could be given. At the end of the lesson Darren pointed out that he had found it impossible to give another smiley face as there was nowhere that met the criteria. The quality of his work was discussed with him and as a result his work returned to the high quality and standard of which he was capable. Using two smiley faces proved a useful strategy, as did the use of prompts to the learners. As these were not all different it was possible to group learners who had similar aspects to work upon and to build this into planning for the next lesson. The learners became more aware of work that was good and could see there were opportunities to improve. They enjoyed the personal feedback and focusing the assessment on the learning intention, and using symbol marking took less than an hour for all the books. On some occasions the prompt given to move the learning forward was actually related to the learners' science target, for example, *the ability to see patterns and trends in graphs and graphical representation.*

Another effective assessment strategy in science is marking by questions. At the end of the lesson the teacher writes a question at the bottom of the work. The learner is challenged to provide an answer at the beginning of the next lesson. Teachers using this approach found that they were providing similar questions for the different abilities of the learners and began to keep a record or bank of questions they could use in the future. These questions were reviewed by the science subject leader and related to the level descriptions. This ensured all learners, but particularly the more able learners, were appropriately challenged. The learners' responses to the questions were very positive and HMI, in a follow-up inspection report, commented favourably on this assessment feedback for the learners. Learners can also mark their own work and can effectively assess their own understanding prior to the teacher marking the work.

Summative Judgements

Formative assessment is vital to help progress learners' learning, however at some points in time a summative judgement is needed to report to others. The National Curriculum in Action site, www.ncaction, provides some examples of work that has been assessed and levels awarded. This is a useful starting point for teachers in schools and for sharing investigative work. Levelling work and justifying why it is, for example, a Level 1, a Level 3 or a Level 5, enables professional judgement to be improved, and this can only be good for learners' learning. Over the past seven years, working in many schools and classrooms carrying out demonstration lessons in investigative science, a major weakness observed is the lack of Level 5 work in investigative settings. Scrutinising many books has demonstrated considerable over-teaching of subject knowledge often to Level 6 and beyond but with limited development of skills and procedural understanding other than a focus on the fair test.

Recording Systems and Testing

Ongoing assessment recording systems, of up and down arrows, helps with future planning because it identifies individual and groups of learners where the pitch of learning has to be adjusted. However, it is also important that teachers plan observation and discussion time with learners. Having a simple way to record the outcome of these activities has challenged teachers. Post-it notes to mark places in learners' work are used by many Foundation Stage teachers, however, these can fall off and get confused with other things, making them less useful. Self-adhesive address labels pre-printed with the learner's name kept on a clipboard, enables notes to be made during lessons. The labels are then transferred directly to the learner's record. One advantage of this system is that it identifies learners for whom no assessment has been recorded because their label remains on the sheet at the end of the week. These learners are often those who are 'average', quiet or just clever at avoiding attention. Some teachers will still want a tick list, showing those learners who can perform certain tasks or who know certain things. Ticks need to be evaluated, judged and, hopefully, acted upon to ensure appropriate learning for learners and, at the end of the unit of work, used to enable a summative judgement to be made. Decisions need to made as to whether these tick lists need to be passed to colleagues and will they want or use them A card system that is accessible to teachers or teaching assistants is useful. There is a card for each learner, stored alphabetically. As a lesson proceeds the appropriate card can be taken and comments with a date added. Similarly, systems that allow learners to consider and record their own achievements are very successful. Learners have sheets with statements to colour or tick when they are ready. The sheet contains statements such as 'I can use a thermometer', 'I can measure accurately' or 'I know what gravitational attraction is'. (Figure 6.2) Teachers also use colour-coded plans: red for not known/covered; yellow for some understanding; and green for clear understanding. Recording takes time and is only worthwhile if the judgements are used to inform future planning. This is especially true when there is regular testing of learners and scores are recorded: 'What do they mean?'

Testing is a disturbing feature because so much science time is being used on such activities and rarely do teachers discuss responses with learners to help extend learning. The cost of tests is also an aspect that should be borne in mind. The direct costs, of providing, administering, invigilating, marking and reporting tests and examinations in primary and secondary schools was estimated at £370m in 2003 in a survey carried out for the QCA by PriceWaterhouseCoopers. The 2007 figure is probably at least twice this, since costs increased by over 70 per cent between 2003 and 2006. (Harlen, 2007).

The Post Note report (POST, 2003) suggested that national testing and the resulting impact of 'teaching to the test' may be one of the features of learners' disaffection and lack of enjoyment of science. In addition there is no evidence that testing improves learners' understanding (ARG, 2002) or that tests are valid or fair (Harlen, 2007).

Analysing tests and looking at whether questions are answered correctly or not will provide some information about aspects that might be improved by adjusting teaching and learning. Such changes usually only benefit the next cohort of learners because those taking the tests have moved on. Teachers could use outcomes of tests more beneficially by spending time post-test discussing with learners the decisions they made and how they would respond if asked a similar question in the future. Here everyone benefits from sharing ideas.

Evaluation

Whatever systems are in place they need evaluating. Planning and pitching lessons is vital and yet it is recording the outcomes that is often the focus of attention. This is counterproductive and focuses upon systems not learners. A system that enables judgements to be made and moderated across a school but that has flexibility in the collection and collation arrangements is desired. It is important that the assessment information is shared with learners. Common reporting formats are needed within a school to enable the summative judgements to be transferred

 Summary

Assessment comprises a number of processes and starts with planning. The long-term experiences need to relate to the learners' needs, and repetition of activities needs to be removed. Challenging learners to improve by pitching lessons appropriately and involving them in the process is essential. Learners need to understand the learning intentions and be involved in the whole process, as learning is not something that can be done *to* others. Learning needs to be thought out in advance with each lesson building upon the last and opportunities provided for learning and not just completion. Feedback should highlight success but also be a guide for the future, and summative judgements should be made in a way that is consistent and meaningful so that in the next year learning continues seamlessly.

Further Reading

Harlen, W. (2007) *Designing a fair and effective assessment system.* Paper presented at the 2007 BERA Annual Conference as part of the ARG symposium Future Directions for Student Assessment.

Swaffield, S. (ed.) (2008) *Unlocking Assessment.* London:Taylor & Francis Ltd.

Warwick P., Linfield, R.S., Stephenson, P. (1999) 'A comparison of primary school pupils' ability to express procedural understanding in science through speech and writing', *International journal of Science Education* 1999, 21: 8, 823–38.

Science from Stories

Claire Hewlett

Introduction

Stories, both true and imaginary, can offer a rich source of learning opportunities for learners of all ages. The traditional folk tale, myths and legends and modern stories that deal with the world in which people live can all be used as a stimulus for supporting learning across a range of curriculum subject, including scientific investigation, as well as provide an everyday starting point for science. This chapter considers why stories should be used as a resource and how fiction can be used to develop scientific understanding, with a particular emphasis on the 7–11 age range (Key Stage 2). A range of practical investigations is suggested as a starting point to illustrate how scientific investigation might be linked to a selection of popular learners' literature.

Why Use Fiction?

Fiction, which also includes poetry, provides learners with opportunities to make connections between scientific concepts and their own life experiences by providing a frame of reference on which to base their learning. Stories provide a vehicle to link previously learnt concepts with new ideas. Good stories have the potential to motivate learners by making them feel involved through the linking of their own understanding of the world to the characters within the book.

With new initiatives in teaching being encouraged, such as the proposals outlined within the Department for Education and Skills' *Excellence and Enjoyment* (DfES, 2003) documentation, teachers are being expected to consider ever more creative ways of delivering the curriculum. Established research has shown that people learn in different ways and for different reasons, and using fiction as a teaching resource enables the teacher to encourage and support a range of different learning styles. It could also be argued that teachers who consciously plan lessons or topics around the use of stories are more likely to adopt a range of different teaching styles themselves in order to meet the needs of the class. The stories chosen in this chapter provide examples of how to interpret the curriculum in different ways in order to provide learners with a stimulating and varied range of lessons that will involve them in their own learning.

Teachers involved in teaching Key Stage 1 regularly use stories both as a starting point and as a stimulus for teaching a range of curriculum subjects, including science. An impressive range of texts, often beautifully and imaginatively illustrated, that explore the world of the child are widely available. Texts such as *The Hungry Caterpillar* by Eric Carle, or *The Enormous Turnip* by Alexi Tolstoy, are standard texts found in the book-corners of many infant classrooms, and learners have opportunities to enjoy these stories on many levels.

This good practice tends largely to disappear in the Key Stage 2 classroom, where teachers are less likely to utilise fiction as a resource within their science teaching. There are possibly several reasons for this; stories are longer and more complex, so finding a story that suits a particular teaching need may be difficult. For the same reason it may be problematic to find a story that appeals to all the learners in the class, or one which allows for continuity and progression within a topic area. With pressure on teachers to deliver a broad and balanced curriculum, they may feel there is not the time to spend reading a story as well as completing a scheme of work, that getting too involved in the story might result in losing the science. However, as the science content at Key Stage 2 becomes more abstract, some of these ideas can be far removed from learners' own experiences and understanding. Providing a context that learners can relate to can help to make the learning more meaningful.

There are obvious solutions. It is not always necessary to read a complete text. Initially a story could be retold in a summarised form to provide the overall context, with relevant chapters then selected to provide the stimulus for further investigation. Another possibility would be to use a text that has been read before that the learners are familiar with, perhaps from another lesson, literacy being the obvious example. Also, it is not always necessary to be tied by the constraints of age-appropriate texts. Many picture books aimed at the younger reader introduce scientific ideas very simply but the underlying concepts are, in fact, quite complex and therefore the material is also relevant for older learners. For example, a story such as *Mommy Laid an Egg* by Babette Cole introduces the concept of reproduction in an accessible way to younger learners but could also be used for teaching about life processes at the 7–11 age range. One of the characteristics of stories for this younger age range is that they are often very humorous, and this can be an added advantage when teaching older learners, helping them to feel more at ease when discussing issues they may feel embarrassed or worried about.

When thinking about what text might be suitable, it is important to be aware that fiction can be used in different ways and for different purposes. Think about the intention. It may be that the aim is to draw out the learners' interest in a story to stimulate and develop lines of enquiry to do with a particular area of study, for example electricity or forces. Alternatively, the aim could be to encourage the learners to solve scientific problems within the story setting that certain characters have encountered, for example, 'Can we make a bridge to help the Three Billy Goats Gruff cross the river?' The story may come first with the science developing from it, or vice versa with the science prompting the selection of a relevant text. Some stories may lend themselves to a range of ways they can be used while others are very specific. A text such as *Danny the Champion of the World* by Roald Dahl provides plenty of opportunity for problem-solving activities to be undertaken in the classroom, while also lending itself to supporting more particular areas of study such as the study of materials or forces. *Old Bear* by Jane Hissey, on the other hand, tends to focus on one thing and therefore could be used specifically as a starting point for an investigation, in this case looking at parachutes.

Developing Science from Stories

Whichever story is chosen, and for whatever reason, it is important to remember not to get overly involved in the text and carried away. Research has found that teachers plan for far more than they ever teach, so they should make sure it is clear how the story is to be used and how it will be integrated into the science teaching. Think about how progression and continuity will be planned for. Read the story and decide whether it covers concepts, skills or attitudes. Then read the story, or the relevant part of the story, with the learners and explore their areas of interest. From these initial 'idea showers' decide upon the investigations and focus upon particular targets.

The following points should help when focusing on planning:

- What exactly will the learners be doing?
- How will they be doing it?
- Why do it? (What skills, concepts or attitudes are you hoping to develop?)
- Is the activity appropriate? (Matching needs, abilities, previous learning.)
- What organisation will be needed?
- What resources, materials, equipment will be needed?
- Safety awareness?

Selecting Stories for Starting Science

The following stories illustrate how texts can be used to support the teaching of science by providing interesting starting points for investigative science. Many of the activities are aimed at Key Stage 2 in order to demonstrate how abstract concepts might be supported, but many of the activities, and indeed the texts themselves, could be adapted for learners younger than this.

Stig of the Dump by Clive King   (1963) Puffin Books   This modern classic about a cave boy transported into the modern world encompasses many areas of the science curriculum, including the overarching requirements

of the nature of scientific ideas. This story has great potential for investigating concepts within the science curriculum and also for developing cross-curricular links to other subjects, in particular design and technology, art and music. The suggestions included here address several areas of the programmes of study so this story could be used to teach any one of these.

Materials and their properties

> He crawled through the rough grass and peered over. The sides of the pit were white chalk, with lines of flint poking out like bones in places. At the top was crumbly brown earth and the roots of the trees that grew on the edge. Some of the trees hung over the edge, holding on desperately by a few roots ... Barney wished he was at the bottom of the pit. And the ground gave way. (pp.2–3)

Taken as a stimulus for work on materials, a suitable starting point might be studying rocks and soils, then moving on to looking at changing and separating materials. Activities could include:

- Starting with some careful observational work: adopt a rock or pebble; memorise the characteristics of the pebble by observation of the size, shape, mass, texture, colour. Can learners identify their own rock when all the rocks are grouped together? Rocks and soils can be investigated further by testing the hardness of different rocks – scratch test – and testing for permeability. Can the learners devise their own investigations to do this?
- What is soil? Can the class make soil? Design and make a wormery (D&T links). Learners could consider how Stig might filter his drinking water.
- Changing materials can be investigated by undertaking activities such as making fossils. Use Plasticine to make casts from shells, fossils or leaves then pour in a plaster of Paris mix. This activity could be a starting point for investigating reversible and non-reversible changes.

Look at pictures of cave paintings: is it possible to produce rock paintings using different soils or by extracting colour from fruit or vegetables?; consider how charcoal is made; draw with chalk and charcoal.

Forces and motion

> The slab of rock was lying flat on the ground. Twelve men with pointed stakes pushed them under the edge of the rock and levered it about a foot off the ground ... The men with the poles and ropes made ready again. This time it was different: because of the steepness of the slope they couldn't pull from the front, but had to do all the lifting and pushing from behind. (pp.152–4)

This section really lends itself to the investigation of forces, in particular studying pulling and lifting, and exploring concepts such as friction and gravity. There is great potential for problem-solving here by presenting learners with some open-ended questions that relate to the characters in the story and that provide opportunities for a wide range of investigative work, for example:

- What happens when more stones have to be pulled up a slope?
- What happens to the force needed as the mass increases?
- What happens when the slope is steeper?
- Where would most force be needed if moving a stone up a slope: in the front or behind?
- Which surface makes moving the stones easiest?
- What is the best way to lift or lever a stone off the ground?

This sort of questioning encourages learners to plan fair test investigations and think about how they will record their results in a systematic manner (a planning format would work very well here). Practical work on pulling and lifting, using stones, containers, slopes, different surface materials and Newton meters, will help to develop conceptual understanding of friction and gravity. Learners could start by investigating what happens when the weight of the stones in a container is increased when the container is pulled along a flat surface. Are there any patterns in their results? What can they conclude? Learners could then progress to investigate the effect of slopes by pulling a fixed mass up different gradients. Can they first predict what might happen? Can they explain their reasoning? Still using the same basic equipment, they could move on to explore the concept of friction and look at how different surfaces affect the pulling force.

Although using levers and pivots is not a requirement of the National Curriculum for science in the junior school, this type of investigation does allow for work on gravity and friction to be extended further and is well within the capabilities of upper junior learners. How might a very simple lever mechanism help to move a stone or help stand a stone upright? A simple way of demonstrating this principle is by using a wooden ruler balanced over a pencil, like a see saw, and placing a heavy object on one end. By exerting pressure with a finger on the other end, learners can explore what happens when the pencil, or fulcrum, is moved nearer to or further away from finger or object. The story ends with the characters at Stonehenge. Learners could then develop their ideas further to investigate how they might move or lift stones to create a small-scale Stonehenge in the school grounds.

Light and sound: the Earth and beyond

[A]nd over the shoulder of the downs appeared a red spark, and the valley was flooded with light. It was sunrise. From the low mist in the bottom of the valley appeared the spire of a church, the tops of oast houses and electricity pylons. (p.156)

This part of the story provides an opportunity to tie this work in with Earth and beyond, particularly looking at day and night, or as a stimulus for exploring the concept of light. Their small-scale model of Stonehenge could be used to investigate shadow formation and they could track the movement of the sun during a school day and look at how shadows can be used to tell the time.

The Iron Man by Ted Hughes   (1968) Faber and Faber   Materials and their properties: physical processes – electricity, forces and motion. This dramatic story lends itself in particular to topic work on electricity and magnetism, and the exploration of metallic materials and their properties:

> The gulls took off and glided down low over the great iron head that was now moving slowly out through the swell. The eyes blazed red, level with the wave tops, till a big wave covered them and foam spouted over the top of the head. The head still moved out under water. The eyes and the head appeared for a moment in a hollow of the swell. Now the eyes were green. (pp.17–18)

The links to metal and magnetic properties tie this activity into science in everyday life. Learners could begin by exploring the properties of different metals and considering the different uses of metals. They could then test different metals for their magnetic qualities and record their findings in simple charts or tables. Questions such as 'Are metals with magnetic properties still attracted to magnets through different materials such as card, water or fabric?' could be answered. Get the learners to plan different ways of testing the strength of a range of magnets. Is strength related to size? Results could be recorded in a variety of charts or tables devised by the learners on the computer.

What would be the best metal for the Iron Man to have been made of? What happens to iron when exposed to salt water? Technically, looking at rusting is no longer in the National Curriculum but it could be included as part of the breadth of study requirements and it does provide opportunities for learners to plan their own fair test investigations if they explore what makes iron nails rust. Rusting is a major economic cost to the industrialised world. Is it possible to prevent rusting? Here would be a good opportunity to place primary school science within the bigger picture.

Stories can often give rise to misconceptions regarding scientific concepts, as the need for dramatic effect often takes precedence over scientific fact. During this story the Iron Man's rusty exterior turns back to shiny rust-free metal. Is this possible in the manner in which it is told? These kinds of misrepresentations in stories could be the basis of investigative work and used to challenge learners' knowledge and understanding. Learners can try to solve the problem of the characters either from the Iron Man's point of view or from that of the villagers.

The changing colours of the Iron Man's eyes are referred to several times throughout the story. Besides looking at how to construct simple circuits and switches, learners always find experimenting with flashing light bulbs in circuits fascinating. What makes the bulb flash? What will happen to another bulb in a series circuit when a flashing bulb is included? Again open-ended questioning can be used to get the learners exploring for themselves and coming up with hypotheses about the flow of electricity around a circuit. Make either a two-dimensional or three-dimensional model of the Iron Man's head, or look further at robots and make a whole iron man from construction kits or from suitable materials. Can the learners make a model where the eyes flash different colours or flash on and off for a fixed period of time? Can they make the eyes flash alternately or alter the brightness of the eyes? Upper Key Stage 2 learners could investigate simple variable resistors in order to do this.

Dr Dog by Babette Cole   Sagebrush

Life processes and living things

This book, aimed at the 4 to 8 age range, uses a medical pretext to indulge the reader in a range of outrageous scatalogical jokes. As with many of her other books there is some serious teaching underpinning the humorous and somewhat ridiculous storyline, in this instance the dangers of smoking and unhealthy eating and the importance of washing hands to prevent spreading germs. Again, it is a story that could be enjoyed by learners in Key Stage 2 as well as by younger learners. This is a fun resource to support the teaching of life processes and to reinforce the concept that all living things need to undertake several processes in order to live. Learners are often confused about life processes and what these involve, even at the end of Key Stage 2, and stories can help to make these more explicit when studying either plants or animals.

The danger of smoking is part of the Key Stage 2 programme on drug awareness. The effect of smoking on the lungs could link to other work on life processes, in particular the importance of exercise and the role of the lungs within the circulatory system, and there are plenty of opportunities for practical work, for example comparing lung capacity. Comparison questions such as 'Do taller learners have a bigger lung capacity?' or 'Do learners with longer legs jump further, run faster?' could be investigated.

Grandpa's rather distasteful eating habits could provide a starting point for work on nutrition and the need for a healthy and varied diet. Learners can survey what their classmates bring in their lunch boxes, keep a food diary, plan a healthy meal for the Grandpa character in the story. How the body can be affected by poor diet could be explored through looking at the function and care of teeth or, again, linked to work on health and fitness. Investigate how much hidden sugar is in someone's daily diet by reading the ingredients on packaging. With older juniors, studying packaging can be a helpful way of learning about micro-organisms. More universal issues could be considered, such as how poor diet affects children in other countries.

Understanding the digestive system is not a requirement in the curriculum for the 7 to 11 age range, but learners are often fascinated by the journey of their food through the body and have no problems with understanding the processes involved if taught to their own level. Taking basic scientific information as a stimulus for creative writing, or just as a means to record

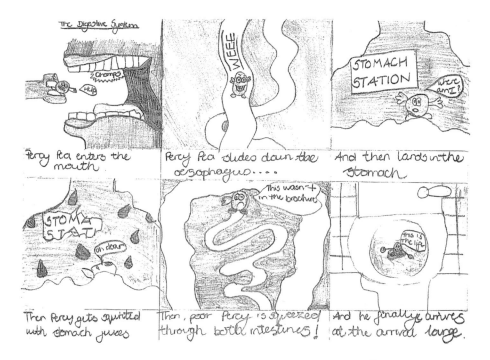

Figure 7.1   The digestive process

what has been learnt, can be very productive. The digestive process is an exciting story in its own right and lends itself to imaginative 'adventure' story writing (Figure 7.1). Getting learners to write their own science stories and poems provides opportunities for self-expression and provides an interesting diversion from the more formal formats often used when writing up a science investigation. (See Chapter 5, p. 67). The digestion story also makes a useful starting point for drama and could be used as the basis for a role-play drama and presented to other learners. Posters and health warnings can also be used to convert the findings of an investigation and be displayed in the classroom or around the school. These are particularly effective when used to support work on life processes, for example, personal hygiene to prevent the spreading of germs, or healthy diet to promote growth, healthy teeth and bones.

Figures 7.2 and 7.3 provide some further suggestions for how fiction might be used as a starting point for science when exploring the environment or looking at forces based on a topic on flight. Both figures include many activities or investigations that can be adapted across the 5 to 11 age range, though some are specifically targeted at an appropriate age range. The stories selected represent a very small sample of the wide range of fiction available to support science teaching. Texts aimed at the 5 to 8 age range are also generally suited to the teaching of concepts with older junior-aged learners.

Figure 7.2   Further suggestions for use of fiction as a starting point in science

Over the Steamy Swamp by Paul Geraghty	Superb illustrations that bring to life the world of a swamp.
Tadpoles Promise by Jeanne Willis and Tony Ross	Embodies life cyles of frogs and butterflies as a tadpole and a caterpillar fall in love with dire consequences
The Tiny Seed by Eric Carle	One of several books by this well known author that teaches about life processes.
Diary of a Worm by Doreen Cronin	Hilarious retelling of a worm's life from his own perspective.
Our Field by Berlie Doherty and Robin Bell Corfield	Three children make an exciting discovery in their summer holidays.
The Secret Garden by Frances Hodgson Burnett	A secret garden, walled, locked and forgotten. Can it be brought back to life? A children's classic.

Careful observation of the environment. Take young children on nature walks and mini safaris to look for things, e.g. flowers with 3/4/5/6 petals, plants that match colours on a paint palette, leaves with different textures, shapes, etc. Trees are plants but are often left out of the curriculum – adopt a tree, what lives in your tree, how tall is your tree, measure the girth withnon standard measurements, how does it change throughout the year?

Cross-sections or transects of a chosen area enable children to observe very carefully what is iving in different areas, e.g. under a tree, by a path, near a hedge in the middle of the field. Again suitable for 5 to 7 age range, older children can record random sampling using hoops or ropes to mark a small area, what is living within? What conclusions can be drawn?

Classify plants and animals by their different features by recording observations in table form. The 7 to 9 age range can identify locally occurring plants and animals and assign to groups using simple keys, older juniors can make their own. Grow plants – beans in jam jars against blotting paper allows children to see the root system develop, suitable for a range of ages particularly 7 to 9-year-olds. Devise a database.

Pond dipping – find out about life cycles of insects. What lives in the bottom, middle, on the surface of the pond? Use keys to classify different insects. What type of plants live in a pond, at the edge of a pond? Look at interdependence between plants and animals. Compare the habitat of the pond with another area around the school.

Design a small wildlife area for your school, what conditions could you provide for plants and animals? Consider the life processes, what is necessary for plants and animals to survive. Undertake a survey to establish living conditions of snails, woodlice or earthworms. Use secondary sources to answer questions that arise when observing living things. Design a home for some woodlice so they can be kept in the classroom.

Children in the 9 to 11 age range can **identify simple food chains in an ecosystem**. Food chain game – children get to be something (e.g. sun, grass, cow, man) and have to put themselves in order. Record food intake from yesterday. All food comes from plants or animals, find out where your food comes from to develop simple food chains (links with geography). Write a dramatic food chain story or act it out as a drama.

Older juniors can explore **food webs and develop the concept of food chains**, some animals eat different things, e.g. herons will eat other things besides fish. Use secondary sources to develop ideas about ecosystems, contrast food webs from Britain with webs from other habitats/ecosystems (*Over the Steamy Swamp*, though aimed at the 5 to 7 age range is an excellent resource for older pupils). Link children together with string to show these complex links. Look at a food chain starting with a mosquito and ending with man, what are the implications? What happens when disease wipes out something in the food chain?

Figure 7.3   Further suggestions as a starting point for use of section 2 in science

Old Bear by Jane Hissey	Old bear has been stored in the attic, can his toy friends think of a way of getting him down?
Flat Stanley by Jeff Brown	Stanley Lambchop awakes one day to find he has been flattened. Various adventures follow including being flown like a kite.
The Eagle and the Wren by Jane Goodall	A tale about flight and how a tiny wren outwits a mighty eagle.
Danny Champion of the World by Roald Dahl	Much loved tale about a boy and the relationship he has with his father. Making a hot air balloon and flying kites are included in two chapters.
The Blue Between the Clouds by Stephen Wunderli	A novel about a friendship between two boys and their mutual passion for flight.

Many of these activities can be adapted for children of different ages:

Drop a weight from different heights into a sand tray. Predict what will happen first. Will there be any difference to the depth of the imprint? What will happen if the height of the drop is altered? Younger children could investigate this and observe what happens, older junior age children could hypothesise before testing.

Drop a screwed up ball of paper and a flat piece of paper from the same height, what happens? What happens if two similar size containers are dropped from the same height simultaneously, one empty and one filled with Plasticine?

Drop items that are made out of the same materials but are different shapes, what happens? Predict which will fall the slowest and give reasons why?

Make kites, paper planes, spinners or parachutes. Investigate which stay in the air the longest, travel the furthest, are the most aerodynamic, etc. (adapt the following investigations). Again, younger children could observe what happens whilst older juniors can develop their own investigations by raising their own questions, identifying variables, thinking about how they might record their results. Explore questions such as:

Parachutes:

• Are some materials better than others for making parachutes?
• Why does a parachute come down slowly?
• What happens if there is a hole in the centre?
• What happens with more than one hole, which is the best number of holes, does the size of the hole make a difference?

Spinners:

• Investigate the factors that keep a spinner in the air for the longest time. What can be changed, measured, recorded? For example, number of wings, length, shape, material. Do they fly better when weighted?
• Look for patterns in results.

Draw pictures showing the direction of the forces with arrows.

Look at birds and how they soar on thermals.

Look for photographs of early attempts at flight and compare some of the factors to those discovered in a paper aeroplane contest.

Links with mathematics; find out how much fuel an aeroplane consumes, work out how much is consumed on set journeys.

Summary

This chapter has considered how fiction can be used as a vehicle to support learning in science. By linking previously learnt concepts with new ideas, fiction can provide a frame of reference on which to base future learning. Fiction provides opportunities for making connections between scientific concepts and learners' own life experiences. Making only small changes to existing planning and practice, to include more use of a wide range of fiction, can enable teachers actively to promote learners' creativity and respond to their creative ideas and actions. Fiction is a powerful and readily available resource to support and engage learners with their own scientific understanding. Good stories have the potential to motivate learners by involving them through linking their own understanding of the world to the characters within the book. Specific examples from well-known learners' literature have been presented to illustrate ways in which fiction might be used as a science resource to support a range of teaching and learning styles. Further suggestions for development are included in Tables 7.1 and 7.2. The chapter has also briefly explored how learners might develop their own self-expression through writing about their science understanding in a variety of ways.

Further Reading

Butzow, C.M. and Butzow, J.W. (2000) *Children's literature in science education*. Libraries Unlimited

Using Role-play to Stimulate and Develop Learners' Understanding of Scientific Concepts

Julie Foreman

Introduction

This chapter will include a brief overview of the theory underlying the use of the whole body, in kinaesthetic experiences, to promote learners' learning in science. Role-play will then be explored as a kinaesthetic tool to promote primary school learners' understanding of abstract scientific concepts. Throughout the chapter the importance of teachers modelling this approach will be emphasised, along with the importance of providing opportunities for learners to practise role-play as a valuable tool of learning. Incorporating role-play with relevant talk will ensure that learners' understanding is developed effectively. Practical suggestions for work in the classroom will follow. Finally, to raise awareness and to avoid misrepresentation, the limitations of the use of role-play will be highlighted.

Teaching Approaches in the National Curriculum

The National Curriculum (DfEE, 1999, p.83) encourages teachers to adopt a flexible approach to teaching science when it states that learners should be taught 'that science is about thinking creatively to try to explain how living and non-living things work'. Therefore, learners should be encouraged to use their imagination and develop their creativity in science lessons. This view is echoed in the more recent *Excellence and Enjoyment: A Strategy for Primary Schools* (DfES, 2003) and is particularly important throughout the primary years.

Some would argue that imagination, rather than knowing facts, is the most important factor needed to learn science and, therefore, the use of imagination should be reflected in its teaching. Without doubt, science is an integral part of modern culture and must aim to stretch the imagination and creativity of young people. The ability to think creatively is an essential attribute of the successful scientist. Therefore learners should be given the opportunity to respond to aspects of science in an imaginative and a creative way. This is especially important if it is to nurture future scientists, since both creativity and an ability to communicate ideas clearly to others are important characteristics of successful scientists.

The implications of this for primary science teaching are huge. Recent OfSTED reports have highlighted that teachers must challenge learners of all abilities, particularly the most able, much further than at present, and that learners need to experience more complex forms of learning. After all, it is generally accepted that learners can achieve more if they are challenged in a non-threatening, motivating way.

While it might be that traditional approaches to teaching science may not stifle creativity in some learners, it is well known that many people have been put off science in the past by their own experience of science in school. However, it is easy to accept that the development of an individual's creativity in science may well be dependent upon the quality and diversity of the learning opportunities provided in the classroom. In fact, it has been found that if too few opportunities are provided for learners to show curiosity then their motivation to engage in creative behaviour can easily be dampened. So, it is important to approach activities in a creative way, ensuring that risk and exploration are encouraged.

Writers on the subject believe that the brain thrives on diversity, so there is a need for the provision of diverse teaching and learning strategies. Learners learn in different ways all the time, and there is no one 'right' way for all. Therefore teachers need to draw upon a variety of different approaches in their teaching to cater for the variety of learners' learning styles.

Research tells us that active learning approaches such as role-play, which engage the intellect in enjoyable, less threatening ways, should play a much larger part in science education than they have in the past. The self-perpetuating saying 'I hear and I forget; I see and I remember; I do and I understand', shows the importance of practical activities. Role-play is one such practical, creative experiential teaching technique (Van Ments, 1983, pp.14–23). Research findings indicate that role-play, as a form of physical modelling, can help learners to visualise and understand abstract scientific concepts. Here, understanding comes not only through participants' high level of involvement, but also through exposure to ideas, discussion and collaboration with other learners.

Role-play has been shown to build upon learners' natural enjoyment of play and can provide much fun and real interest. Role-play can be considered to be a very natural learning medium when one considers how much time very young learners engage in undirected, imaginative, fantasy play both in their own play outside school and, when given the opportunity, in the nursery and Early Years classroom. This natural tendency to engage in role-play can be harnessed by the teacher in a more structured way to encourage learning about aspects of science. What is more, role-play is motivational because it involves activity and provides a break from established classroom routines.

Movement can represent or exemplify what cannot easily be put into words (Bruner and Haste, 1993, p.169). Therefore, since role-play involves physical movement, it can be used to help to explain abstract concepts. Recent research into how the brain helps to construct learning suggests that movement is potentially an effective teaching strategy in developing lifelong networks of connections in the brain (Smith, 1999, p.33). Here, the human body is considered to be a 'powerful route into learning' (Smith, 1999, p.178). This form of physical learning can be termed as a kinaesthetic learning style, viewed as a 'bodily-kinaesthetic intelligence' by Gardner (1993, p.9). However, role-play demands more than just bodily movement. There is also a need for interaction and collaboration. In this way, the needs of a range of learning styles can be met. Role-play can also be viewed as a valuable learning experience which integrates different areas of the brain (Smith, 1999, p.37). Added to this notion, creative activities such as role-play allow learners not only to communicate using familiar language codes, but may encourage learners to communicate using 'language usually restricted to scientists' (Taylor, 1997, p.39), thereby developing their use of scientific vocabulary.

In order for role-play to be effective in giving an insight into a scientific way of thinking, it is important that the teacher models an idea before it is practised by the learners. To achieve maximum benefit, role-play should be used regularly in science from the earliest days in formal education and throughout the school. In this way, learners become familiar with this strategy and therefore will develop their confidence in participation – confidence being a powerful factor in learning. Familiarisation has been shown to develop learners' ability to use role-play more effectively to show their learning and so provide a form of assessment of their learning. The use of role-play has also been shown to illustrate abstract scientific concepts and to facilitate learners' retention of the knowledge gained.

Role-Play in the Primary School

As stated above, it is important that role-play is incorporated into school schemes of work so that learners can become familiar with this teaching strategy and confident in participation. Role-play is already an important strategy in the early years of schooling, though not necessarily for the development of scientific knowledge and understanding. It is very common for very young learners in school to 'act-out', for example, an extract from books of traditional tales and to engage in more informal role-play in the 'home corner'. It is easy, therefore, to extend this idea to simple scientific ideas at the Foundation Stage. It is easy to link literacy to science in this way. The use of 'props' is important in role-play. Older learners will benefit from the use of labels and pictures during the delivery of their role-play. Younger learners may well 'dress-up', wear masks or dress models to help to communicate scientific ideas.

One difficult concept for younger learners to understand relates to forces, i.e. pushes and pulls. Here, following the reading of *The Enormous Turnip*, small groups of learners can role-play parts of the story to pull the enormous turnip from the ground. In doing so, their understanding of forces will be developed. Similarly, many scientific concepts can be explored through role-play starting with a story, or observation. Older learners can often approach the representation of ideas in a very creative, imaginative way if they are given the opportunity to put forward their own ideas after brief instruction.

Table 8.1 illustrates how other topics can be developed through the use of role-play throughout the school. However, it is important to appreciate that many of

Table 8.1 Aspects of role-play that could develop from different starting points

Topic	Age group	Aspects of role-play
Shoes (Scientific aspect: Materials and their properties)	Foundation Stage	Pupils think about the properties of the materials used for different kinds of footware, e.g. soft warm fabric for slippers, stiff leather for boots and some shoes, flexible materials for beach 'flip-flops' and 'jelly' shoes. Pupils then to act out one of these to demonstrate the properties.
Mini-beasts	Foundation Stage	Following observation of mini-beasts, pupils could pretend to move like different creatures: props could include, e.g. additional limbs to enable pupils to become spiders or insects. A small sleeping bag can make a good 'prop' for the skin of a caterpillar.
Waterproofing	5–6 years	Ideas related to the properties of materials: some materials can let through water others cannot. Pupils enacting the particles of water and different materials.
Day and night	5–6 years	Ideas relating to the movement of the Earth in relation to the Moon and the Sun. Pupils enacting the spin of the Earth in relation to the Sun to show how day and night occur.
Electricity	6–7 years	Push the push: pupils to stand in a circle holding a rope and pass it through their hands to illustrate the flow of electricity. One pupil could act as the light bulb and slow the movement of the rope.
Shadows	7–8 years	Ideas related to how light travels: Some materials allow light to pass through whilst others do not i.e. exploring opaque, translucent and transparent materials. Pupils enacting the path of the light and how it may be reflected, passed through or absorbed by the material in its path.
Thermal insulation	8–9 years	Ideas related to heat transfer: Why ice cream does not melt when wrapped in newspaper and why newspaper keeps chips hot. Pupils representing the heat transfer and the newspaper, i.e. the heat is prevented from passing through the newspaper either from the outside, or the inside of the package.

Topic	Age group	Aspects of role-play
Dissolving	9–10 years	Ideas about solubility: that some things will dissolve in a liquid, whilst others will not. That there is a limit to the amount of substance that will dissolve in a liquid. Pupils acting as the particles of a liquid and the material to be dissolved.
Filtering	9–10 years	Ideas about particle size: that some particles are too big to pass through a filter, whilst others are not. Some pupils acting as the filter letting some particles through, other pupils acting as the particles trying to get through the filter.
Evaporation	9–10 years	Ideas about movement of particles: puddles evaporating. Pupils acting as the particles of a liquid changing to a gas – without boiling.
Sun, Moon and Stars	9–10 years	Ideas relating to the position and movement of planets around the Sun.
Sun, Moon and Earth	10–11 years	Ideas relating to the position and movement of the Earth around the Sun and the Moon around the Earth. Pupils to act as the Sun, Earth and Moon to show the orbits of the Earth and Moon. The same side of the Moon facing its orbit can be enacted and the length of one complete spin of the Earth explained.
Food webs	10–11 years	Pupils acting as the Sun, plants and animals in a number of food chains using string to link them appropriately. Cross-link food chains to show a food web with the Sun at the centre.
Sexual reproduction in plants: pollination	10–11 years	Pupils can take the role of the sex organs of flowering plants such as the stamens and the stigma. One pupil then acts as a pollinator (e.g. a bee) flying from flower to flower.
Making a classification key	10–11 years	All pupils in the class to line up and discuss/develop questions with yes/no answers to group/classify the pupils as in a branching key, e.g. Does the child have blue eyes?
Heart and circulation	10–11 years	See Case Study 8.1

the same ideas can be approached at different ages and abilities. Here, it is the role of the teacher to choose the level of the idea to be explored and to decide how much help to give to learners in formulating the role-play. For example, within the topic of electricity, while younger learners may only be asked to represent the flow of electricity in an electric circuit using a skipping rope, older learners could be expected to role-play, for example, the flow of the electrons, the learners themselves acting as the electrons in a circuit. Concepts such as resistance, series and parallel circuits could then be developed in this way.

 Case Study 8.1

This case study comes from a three-form entry primary school situated in the centre of a small town in the South East of England. The class contained a wide range of abilities with a high proportion of learners with special educational needs. Learners in Year 5 had been undertaking a topic on health and fitness, including learning about the circulatory system. The teacher realised that many learners in the class were confused about this process and she felt that the diagrams in the available non-fiction books were difficult to interpret by many in the class. The teacher decided to involve the learners in a role-play as a way to develop their understanding of the circulatory system. The role-play consisted of the journey of the blood between the lungs and heart. This was used to explain how oxygen and carbon dioxide are transferred to the organs of the body by the blood.

The school, like many others, had a tradition of each class taking turns, each week, to present a class assembly which parents were invited to attend. The class in question, when it was their turn, decided that they would like to present their role-play from earlier in the term. The class were accustomed to making their own decisions about what and how to present their assemblies, so, after initial discussion, the class were left alone to plan for themselves. What resulted was an extended version of their original role-play into a scripted drama that included actions, expressions and dialogue. The narrator, electing to wear a white laboratory coat, goggles and a red wig, and armed with a clipboard and pointing stick, proceeded to act out the role of 'mad scientist'. Whilst explaining the journey of the blood around the body, some of the learners were organs strategically placed around the hall, while the remainder of the learners took the role of the corpuscles. The corpuscles moved around the hall filling up with oxygen in the lungs and slowly running out of oxygen as they moved around the body feeding the organs.

When the class were preparing their 'leavers' service the following year they were asked to write about their favourite memories. The narrator wrote about their play and could still recall the main teaching points he had learned the year before.

The Use of Role-Play in Two Areas of the National Curriculum

The remainder of this chapter will look at the use of role-play in two areas of the curriculum based upon work with a class of Year 5 learners, i.e:

- solids, liquids and gases
- sound.

In each example, the National Curriculum references covered by the role-play within the Programmes of Study will be highlighted. Guidance will be provided to show how role-play can be used to physically model these scientific concepts. Photographs will be included for illustration. Suggestions will be made for points to emphasise during the role-play in order to challenge learners' possible misconceptions. Additionally, this section will outline possible group extension activities to enable learners to use role-play to show their conceptual understanding. Finally, this section will present examples of possible outcomes of using these approaches in the primary science classroom.

It is important, before undertaking any role-play activities, that the issue of scale in relation to learners acting as the particles is clearly explained to them, as we are dealing here with a highly abstract concept.

Solids, Liquids and Gases

What follows are specific suggestions for how learners can be organised to undertake the role-play.

Making a solid

What are you trying to show?

Solids, liquids and gases form part of Sc3 within the National Curriculum, i.e. Materials and their properties. It is expected that 7–11-year-old learners should be taught to recognise differences between solids, liquids and gases, in terms of ease of flow and maintenance of shape and volume.

Learners are to represent particles (atoms and molecules) in the role-play.

(Continued)

(Continued)

Teaching points

- The particles in a solid can only vibrate in fixed positions, they cannot move around because the particles are tightly bound – ask the learners to simulate this by wobbling.
- The solid has a fixed shape and volume. It can change its shape only when another force is applied – this can also be simulated.

What do you need?

Examples of solids for learners to examine their properties. Learners could also bring into school lists of solids investigated at home or on the Internet.

How do you prepare the class?

Learners to investigate a range of solids and establish the properties of a solid.

Running the role-play

Select nine learners to form a solid. Arrange them in rows of three and ask them to link arms as shown in Figure 8.1.

Questions to ask

Before the role play:

If we were to become the particles in a solid (explanation of scale would be needed here), how could we show the properties of a solid?

During the role play:

How can we show that the particles in a solid can only vibrate in fixed positions and cannot move around? How can we show that the particles are tightly bound and a solid has a fixed shape and volume?

After the role play:

Discussion to reinforce the properties of a solid referring to the role-play.

Follow-up work

Learners to record the properties of a solid referring to the role play using a method of their choice, such as:

- cartoon strip
- newspaper article
- poster

- diagram
- story on the life of a solid
- poem.

Further role-plays on liquids, gases and change of state to be covered next.

Figure 8.1   Photograph of learners role-playing a solid

Making a liquid

What are you trying to show?

Solids, liquids and gases form part of Sc3 within the National Curriculum, i.e. Materials and their properties. This states that at Key Stage 2 pupils should be taught to recognise differences between solids, liquids and gases, in terms of ease of flow and maintenance of shape and volume.

(Continued)

(Continued)

Pupils are to represent particles (atoms and molecules) in the role-play.

Teaching points

- The particles are still closely bonded but they can 'slide' around each other in a liquid.
- Liquids can change their shape to fit the container they are in – this can be simulated by 'pouring' the liquid particles into a contained area made by tables or chairs, for example, as shown in the photograph.
- Liquids keep the same volume when they are poured from one container to another. The liquid particles could be 'poured' into another arrangement of chairs, but the number of particles remains the same.

What do you need?

Examples of liquids. Pupils could bring lists of liquids from investigation at home, on the Internet, etc.

How do you prepare the class?

Pupils to investigate a range of liquids to establish the properties of a liquid.

Running the role-play

Select another nine pupils to make a solid again and explain that you are a source of heat to be applied to the solid.

In a solid that will melt, the particles begin to vibrate/wobble faster and they gradually become a liquid when a temperature is reached that causes the particles to vibrate/wobble so fast that they break free of their bonds and begin to flow.

Ask the pupils to 'drop' their linking arms and 'slide' around each other as shown in the photograph (Figure 8.2).

Questions to ask

Before the role play

How can we change a solid to a liquid?

How does a liquid differ from a solid?

If we were to become the particles in a liquid, how could we show the properties of a liquid?

During the role play

How can we show that particles in a liquid are still closely bonded, but can slide around each other?

How can we show that liquids can changed their shape to fit the container they are in, but keep the same volume?

After the role play

Discussion to reinforce the properties of a liquid referring to the role-play. Further comparison of the properties of a solid and liquid.

Follow-up work

Pupils to record the properties of a liquid referring to the role-play using a method of their choice such as:

- Cartoon strip of how a solid changes to a liquid
- Story to describe the journey of a liquid
- Flow diagram of what happens to the particles in a solid as it changes to a liquid
- Poster to compare the properties of a solid and a liquid
- Diary in the life of a solid and how it changes to a liquid

Further role-plays on gases and changes of state to be covered next.

Figure 8.2   Photograph of learners role-playing a liquid

Making a gas

What are you trying to show?

Solids, liquids and gases form part of Sc3 within the National Curriculum, i.e. Materials and their properties. This states that at Key Stage 2 pupils should be taught to recognise differences between solids, liquids and gases, in terms of ease of flow and maintenance of shape and volume, and also about reversible changes, including dissolving, melting, boiling, condensing, freezing and evaporating.

Pupils are to represent particles (atoms and molecules) in the role-play.

Teaching points

- Gases have no fixed shape or volume and they can spread out to fill any space or container – the pupils running around to the extremities of the room space can show this.
- The particles are spread out with nothing between them, moving fast and in all directions – the pupils as particles may occasionally bump into each other and change direction to simulate the gas.
- The particles of a gas can be squeezed into a smaller space – pupils moving from the playground space to the classroom for example can simulate this.
- Warming a gas makes its particles move even faster and further apart, causing them to press harder on the sides of a container or space.

What do you need?

Examples of gases. Pupils could bring lists of gases from investigation at home, from the Internet, etc.

How do you prepare the class?

Pupils to observe and discuss where gases are found to establish the properties of gases.

Running the role-play

Select another nine pupils to make a solid, then a liquid, by warming the solid as before.

This time, by adding more heat, the particles move around each other more easily until they move so quickly that they escape from the surface of the liquid.

Ask the pupils to move very quickly around each other and then one by one leave the 'liquid' and move quickly in random directions around the room space as shown in Figure 8.3.

Questions to ask

Before the role play:

How can we change a solid to a liquid, to a gas?

How does a gas differ from a solid and a liquid?

If we were to become the particles in a gas, how could we show the properties of a gas?

During the role play:

How can we show that particles of a gas can spread out to fill any space or container and have no fixed shape or volume?

How can we show that particles of gas move very fast and in all direction?

How can we show that the particles move even faster when warmed?

How can we show that particles of a gas can be squeezed into a smaller space?

After the role play:

Ask questions to elicit from the pupils what they have learned about the properties of a gas – referring to the role-play in order to reinforce the concepts.

Further comparison of the properties of a solid, liquid and gas.

Follow-up work

Pupils to record the properties of a gas referring to the role-play using a method of their choice, such as:

• Cartoon strip of how a solid changes to a liquid to a gas
• Story of life as a gas particle
• Poster showing a range of gases in everyday life incorporating the properties
• Newspaper article of what happens when a solid changes to a liquid to a gas

Further role-plays, changes of state in everyday life to be covered next.

Possible group extension activities to enable learners to use role-play to show their conceptual understanding

After these illustrative role-play activities learners can be grouped to show through role-play the concepts for assessment purposes and to provide opportunities for presentation and whole-class discussion to clarify any arising misconceptions:

Figure 8.3   Photograph of students role-playing a gas

Possible role-plays	Links to National Curriculum	Instructions on how this can be managed
Evaporation What happens to the water particles in wet hair as a hair dryer is drying it?	• Materials and their properties • Changing materials • Reversible changes • The water cycle	Establish with the pupils the change of state taking place
Evaporation What happens to water particles when water evaporates from a puddle?	• Materials and their properties • Changing materials • Reversible changes • The water cycle	Consider the motion of the particles in each state of matter
Condensation What happens to water vapour in the air as it hits a cold glass of water?	• Materials and their properties • Changing materials • Reversible changes • The water cycle	Ask pupils what happens in the change of state in question – refer to the previously explored role-plays
Melting What happens when chocolate melts?	• Materials and their properties • Changing materials • Reversible changes	Identify in chosen groups who is to act as one of the particles, who is to be the narrator and any other props, e.g. the hairdryer
Freezing What happens to water in an ice cube tray placed in the freezer?	• Materials and their properties • Changing materials • Reversible changes	Groups of pupils then prepare their identified change of state role-play for presentation to the rest of the class
Boiling What happens to a pan of water as it is boiled on the cooker hob?	• Materials and their properties • Changing materials • Reversible changes	

Figure 8.4   How to manage role-plays

Note: It is important to make clear that most substances contract when they change from a liquid to a solid with the exception of water, which expands when it freezes. The learners could be challenged to show this in the freezing role play. Learners could show this when they form the solid in the role–play by holding hands and pushing outwards rather than linking arms to show the bonds as in the previous examples.

Outcomes of using these approaches in the primary science classroom

Knowledge and understanding that matter is made up of particles and their arrangement and movement in solids, liquids and gases is not identified in the Key Stage 2 National Curriculum (DfEE, 1999, p.87) – this concept is identified at a level 6 understanding in Key Stage 3 (DfEE, 1999, p.23), although modelling is identified at level 5. However, research has shown that learners at early secondary age show very little appreciation of the intrinsic motion of particles (Johnson, 1999, p.93). Other research has shown that learners modelling the intrinsic motion of particles can enhance their understanding of the properties of solids, liquids and gases (Foreman, 2002, p.61). Below are some of the responses of a Year 5 class interviewed after taking part in the role-play of solids, liquids and gases:

> I think when I look at solids, liquids and gases I will think of what is going on inside them. (Boy aged 9 years)

> I learned that molecules actually move round, before I didn't know I thought they just stayed still and then if you move them and then they move. (Boy aged 10 years)

> Because we got to do what they (particles) were doing and if you had to write it down you wouldn't know what they would be doing and what it would be like to be them. (Girl aged 9 years)

The learners' class teacher stated that the use of role-play:

> Helped to explain concepts that are very hard to understand. I think that really took them that stage further and also consolidated what they already knew … it stretched them to the limit of what they could assimilate.

These learners were also able to retain the knowledge and understanding attained through the role-play, when questioned at the end of the school year, with responses as follows:

> We went into groups and showed how solids, liquids and gases move and we were the molecules. When the molecules were tightly bonded they were a solid, when they were free and filled all the space they were a gas and when they slide over and around each together they were a liquid. (Girl aged 10 years)

> My group's role-play was when you had washed your hair and you are drying it with the hairdryer. The water started off as a liquid and finished as a gas because the hair was dried. We moved slowly at first but got faster as the hair dried. (Girl aged 10 years)

We could actually do what we felt but when you are writing you can't really do it ... Sometimes I find it hard to put my ideas down. It made it clearer than just normal speaking, because we could actually do it and it would make us understand more. (Boy aged 9 years)

Sound

What are you trying to show?

Sound features in Sc4 of the National Curriculum, i.e. Physical Processes. Here learners should be taught that sounds are made when objects vibrate but that vibrations are not always directly visible. Also they should be taught how to change the pitch and loudness of sounds produced by some vibrating objects and that vibrations from sound sources require a medium through which to travel to the ear.

Use of the role-play

Learners need the experience of representing particles (atoms and molecules) in solids, liquids and gases prior to the role-play activities relating to sound travelling.

Teaching points

- Sound can travel faster through solids than through liquids and faster through liquids than through gases.
- It is the sound wave that moves through the material/medium and not the particles of the material.
- The sound source vibrates and so vibrates the particles of the surrounding materials in the same way and this is how sound travels.
- Sound can only travel through materials, so cannot travel through outer space.

What do you need?

String telephones

Wooden broom handles

Plastic tanks filled with water

Inflated balloons

How do you prepare the class?

Learners should investigate and observe how sound travels through different materials and states of matter (solids, liquids and gases).

Learners can share observations about their experiences of sound travelling in the swimming pool, bath at home, etc.

Sound travelling through a string telephone

Divide the class in halves, so that the learners have the experience of enacting and 'feeling' the role-play and also observing the role-play. Arrange them in a single row with arms placed on the shoulders of the learner in front, as shown in Figure 8.5. The learners need to hold on tightly. Ensure that both halves of the class have both experiences and discuss their observations after the role-play.

You will act as the sound source vibrating, rocking backwards and forwards, so that when you grasp the shoulders of the learner at the end of the line they rock backwards and forwards and in turn they rock the learner in front of them and so on down the line.

Learners will be able to 'feel' the sound wave move down the line, through themselves as particles, and the observing half of the class will be able to see the sound wave move along the particles of the 'string telephone'.

Figure 8.5   Photograph of learners role-playing aspects of sound

Loudness or amplitude

Using the same arrangement as before with the learners as particles in a string telephone with their hands placed on the shoulders of the learner in front, the learners can show the range of loudness by the extent of how far they as particles move backwards and forwards.

(Continued)

(Continued)

- For very loud sounds they can rock backwards and forwards a long way.
- For very quiet sounds they move a little way forwards and backwards.

Teaching points

- Loudness is increased by the size of the vibrations (amplitude) of the sound source being increased, such as hitting a drum harder.

Pitch or frequency

Using the same arrangement as for loudness, the range of pitch can be shown by how quickly the learners as particles move backwards and forwards.

- For very high-pitched sounds they move very quickly backwards and forwards.
- For very low-pitched sounds the learners move more slowly backwards and forwards.

Teaching points

- Pitch or frequency is that rate at which the vibrations go backwards and forwards.
- Small or short vibrating points cause the vibrations to move quickly and so the sounds they produce are high pitched.
- Long or large vibrating points cause the vibrations to move more slowly and so the sounds they produce are low pitched.

Questions to ask

Before the role play:

What is happening to the sound source to create the sound?

When sound travels through a material how does it travel?

What happens to the particles in the material?

What happens to the particles in a loud sound?

What happens to the particles in a quiet sound?

What happens to the particles in a low-pitched sound?

What happens to the particles in a high-pitched sound?

If we were to become a string telephone, how could we show what happens to the particles as sound travels through the string?

During the role play:

Can you feel the sound wave travelling through?

Can you see the sound wave travelling through?

What is happening to the particles in the string telephone as the sound travels?

How can you show a loud sound travelling through the string telephone?

How can you show a quiet sound travelling through the string telephone?

How can you show a high-pitched sound travelling through the string telephone?

How can you show a low-pitched sound travelling through the string telephone?

After the role play:

Referring to role play:

Why do you think sound travels faster through a solid than through a liquid?

Why do you think sound travels faster through a liquid than through a gas?

Follow-up work

Recap on how sound travels, loudness and pitch.

Possible group extension activities to enable learners to use role-play to show their conceptual understanding

Challenge the learners in smaller groups to show the movement of particles in the following concepts:

- A low-pitched, loud sound.
- A high-pitched, loud sound.
- A low-pitched, quiet sound.
- A high-pitched, quiet sound.

Sound travelling through different materials

The concept that sounds can travel faster through a solid, than a liquid, than a gas can also be role-played drawing upon the experiences of the role-plays covered so far. However it may be more beneficial to set this as a group challenge for the learners.

Possible group extension activities to enable learners to use role-play to show their conceptual understanding.

In groups learners can be challenged to show and compare what happens when sound travels through solids, liquids and gases and to explain why travels sound more quickly through solids, than liquids than gases.

Learners will need to draw upon their knowledge of the role-playing of solids, liquids and gases, and how sounds travels from a vibrating sound source of previous role-plays.

Outcomes of using these approaches in the primary science classroom

Almost all the learners who were interviewed after being involved in the sound role-plays were able to 'feel' the sound wave moving, which they considered enhanced their learning. Comments made by the learners included:

> It is easier to remember how sound travels now in the role-play, easier than writing it down. (Boy aged 9 years)

The observation of the role-play was also beneficial for those who could not 'feel' the sound wave moving in the role-play:

> I couldn't really feel the sound wave moving along but I could see it when the others were in the line. (Boy aged 9 years)

Similar to the outcomes discussed earlier, it was also shown that learners were able to retain the knowledge and understanding attained through the sound role-play, when questioned at the end of the school year, with responses as follows:

> I learnt that when sound travelled through the molecules we moved backwards and forwards. We call that movement vibration. (Girl aged 9 years)

> We lined up and put our hands on the person's shoulder in front of you and one person at the back pushed the person in front and everyone moved forwards and backwards and created a sound wave. (Girl aged 9 years)

> When a loud sound hits the molecules they go backwards and forwards a long way. When a quiet sound hits it doesn't go backwards so far. (Girl aged 10 years)

During their associated presentations the following comment was made:

> The tighter the bonds are linked, the faster the sound travels through. (Boy aged 9 years)

When questioned later on in the year the following expression was recorded:

> Sound travels most quickly through a solid because the particles are so tightly packed together that the sound can go through a lot easier for them to bump into them and to let the sound travel through the particles. (Girl aged 10 years)

▢ Summary

This chapter has considered why role-play is an important and appropriate teaching strategy for use in primary science and has explored a number of ideas for use in the classroom. The following provides a number of issues to think about and points of guidance to consider when planning to use role-play in the classroom:

Issues

- Role-play and drama can provide a break from established classroom routines, something learners enjoy.
- Role-play can provide a fun way to focus learners on specific aspects of value in learning.
- The physical modelling as a form of kinaesthetic learning enables learners to understand abstract concepts.
- Role-play is a form of learning, which is accessible by all learners irrespective of ability and learning style.
- Learners are very aware of their own learning and are able to retain scientific concepts through the physical involvement.

Guidance

- Initially there is a need for the teacher to model and intervene to support learners' development of independence, confidence and proficiency in using role-play as a tool to show understanding.
- Grouping learners to devise their own role-plays to show conceptual understanding challenges them through cognitive conflict to develop thinking.
- Learners prefer to use role-play as the method to show their understanding as opposed to writing it down.
- Presentation of the role-play can provide a class with an opportunity to consolidate their own learning and the teacher with an opportunity for assessment.

It is hoped that the examples of role-plays discussed within this chapter and the evidence presented will inspire you to use role-play across the science curriculum to illustrate scientific concepts. What is most important is to consider learners' creativity in devising their own role-plays. Your learners may never cease to amaze you with their imagination and ingenuity!

Further Reading

Littledyke, M. (2001) 'Drama and primary science'. Paper presented at the British Educational Research Association Annual Conference, Leeds University, 13–15 September 2001. The text is in the Education-line internet document collection at: <http://www.leeds.ac.uk/educol/documents/00001858.htm>, 2001, p.9.

Odegaard, M. (2003) 'Dramatic science. A critical review of drama in science education', *Studies in Science Education*, 39, pp.75–101.

Ward, H. (2007) Chapter 4 'Moving and learning', in *Using their brains in science: ideas for children Aged 5 to 14*. London: Sage.

9

Science from Games

Hellen Ward

Introduction

Learners need to be able to use the complex language of science and without this language they may fail to make progress (QCA 2006). Games offer the opportunities for learners to learn both knowledge of science and associated vocabulary in an interesting way. Language acquisition and enjoyment can be promoted effectively through the use of scientific games. With a large number of learners choosing science as their least liked subject, action is needed (Pollard and Trigg, 2000, Beggs and Murphy, 2003, Wellcome Trust, 2005). Reasons given for the learners' lack of interest in science are the need to write formally in science, the focus upon revision, the impact of the national tests and the lack of interesting fun things in the curriculum. There is also a mismatch between teachers' views of science, with more than 80 per cent of primary teachers saying science offered lessons that learners enjoyed, while learners rated science as unpopular. While teachers found the parts of the plants the easiest part of the science curriculum to teach, learners found this the most difficult (Wellcome Trust, 2005). Given that potential future scientists are experiencing science in classrooms all around the UK the question is, 'Are their needs and the future needs of society being met?'

How Can the Use of Games Enrich the Primary Science Curriculum?

Playing games of different types provides a wealth of learning opportunities. Play is known to be a powerful mediator for learning throughout a person's life. Learners select different types of games outside the classroom and they thrive on learning that is challenging:

> Did you ever hear a game advertised as being easy? What is worst about school curriculum is the fragmentation of knowledge into little pieces. This is supposed to make learning easy, but often ends up depriving knowledge of personal meaning and making it boring. Ask a few kids: the reason most don't like school is not that the work is too hard, but that it is utterly boring (Papert, 1998).

This view is one that rings true with many observations of learners who exhibit behaviour problems in the classroom. This is often because 'challenge' and 'play' do not feature as elements of learning in some classrooms and interesting science lessons are not found everywhere. 'They go on and on and when they have finished you do not have enough time to do the work' (Year 3 boy, large rural Local Authority). However, science can be stimulating and memorable with the use of alternative strategies. Chapter 8 puts forward a convincing argument that play and its associated teaching strategies can be used effectively to enhance learning and provide the motivation and long-term development of positive attitudes towards science.

Commonly accepted is the idea that learners have different learning styles. Learning styles have become central to some schools' ways of working with teachers planning visual, auditory and kinaesthetic (VAK) activities predominantly. However, while 'brain gym' and VAK have become popular, the scientific evidence to support their use is not published. Partly, perhaps, this may be because the nature of educational research makes it impossible to isolate all the factors involved in, and that influence, effective learning, and therefore difficult to conclude that it is really 'brain gym' or use of learning styles that make the difference. This means that the casual link between the use of these strategies is almost impossible to identify in normal classrooms. However, research suggests learners enjoy being in those classrooms where a range of approaches are used. This increased enjoyment and motivation have been linked to increases in learning (Dweck, 1999). In order to develop as whole people, all styles and approaches should be included in teaching and learning for all learners (Kolb, 1984).

The benefits of using play as a positive strategy in the classroom can be enormous. However, allowing learners merely to play in order to make an interesting lesson, in itself, is not the answer. Play has to be planned for and managed. In order for play to be used productively, learners must be attentive and on task and the games must be motivating and fun.

To increase positive participation, depending on the games chosen, an element of competition could be introduced. Having a reason or an audience for the activity can enhance motivation. Team games in science are more motivating for all learners, particularly when the teams are made of learners of mixed gender and ability. If the game is designed in a way that encourages learners to improve on past performance then they will be keen to learn vocabulary or concepts and may not even think of it as 'work'. This type of play is a 'win–win' situation, where all learners work together to improve the class time or score rather than one group winning at the expense of the rest of the class. Games can also be good for helping learners with the hard-to-learn facts such

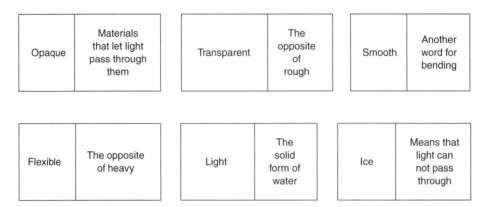

Figure 9.1   Chain games

as the life cycle of plants, and are a good way to bring up complex issues such as drugs or smoking.

Developing Scientific Language through Games: Links to Literacy

Language development is central to learning science, and games that help with this should be encouraged. Bingo, chain (or link) games and matching words and definitions are all easy, fun and enjoyable. Bingo and chain games (Figure 9.1) are most effective if played in mixed ability teams to begin with, rather than all learners having their own cards. These activities can later be used as individual games when confidence and understanding of vocabulary are raised.

Chain games start with one learner or the teacher reading the first question, the answer being provided on a card somewhere else in the room. The person with the correct answer then reads their question and so the chain (or link) is made. It is important that the words used are discussed with the class since learners may suggest more than one answer and the precision of word usage is one of the most difficult aspects of science for learners to develop.

Subject-specific bingo (Figure 9.2), for example, on forces, helps learners to be exposed to scientific vocabulary and promotes learning by immersion. Vocabulary development is always an area where learners need help, and regular immersion for short periods of time is more beneficial to learning than exposure only once a week. Lemke (1990, p.24) suggested that learning science was like learning a foreign language, where immersion and regular involvement enhance understanding and proficiency. Usually in bingo, gaining a 'full house' is the target, but here, because of time constraints, learners could play just for one line. In this case, the teacher selects words according to the scientific topic under study and reads the definitions to the learners. Although many games of this type are commercially produced, these can be made easily and cheaply using index cards. In this way, the game can be tailored to the different needs of specific learners and can make these ideas accessible to all.

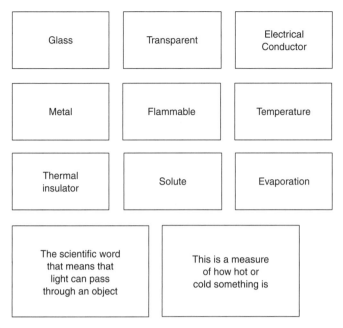

Figure 9.2   Bingo

Scientific 'hangman' can develop learners' visual vocabulary. When the word is guessed the learners can gain extra marks from the teacher if they can define the term accurately. Here there is room for further discussion and exploration of the meaning of terms and so, in the long term, learners will become more able to define terms accurately.

'I can think of three' is a quick and easy game to encourage learners to use their thinking skills; for example, 'Name three solids that are opaque'. To increase the demand, older learners in groups could be asked to think of as many opaque solids as they can in three minutes. At the end of the time the group that has been able to think of the greatest number can be selected to share their ideas first. This enables common answers to be discussed. Other groups can then add any additional examples that the first group has not included. This discussion develops the links in the learners' brains and will remind them of things that they already know (Ward, 2007). The fact that there is not one answer also makes the learners think creatively. The debate and discussion that follows these activities are as important as the list generated, as discourse is found to improve learners' national tests scores (Mant, Wilson and Coates 2007). An example of this was provided by a group of Year 6 learners who had a very lively debate on the state of matter of toothpaste as a result of the above challenge.

Crosswords and word searches have always been used extensively in science, along with cloze procedures. When churned out in worksheet format the focus of the lesson can easily be lost and so can the fun. This does not have to be the case. If crosswords are produced on an interactive whiteboard, an effective lesson starter can be created. Learners can then work together, for example, some groups solving the across clues whilst others focus upon the down clues. This

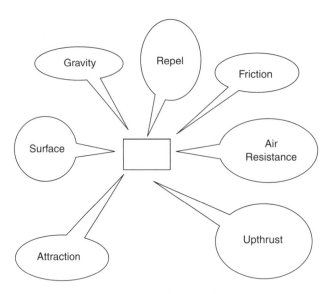

Can you give me a question for each of these answers?

Figure 9.3 'What's the question?' challenge sheet

is an easy way to introduce differentiation and helps learners not only with the development of vocabulary, but also with the spelling of scientific words, i.e. if the words are spelt incorrectly they will not fit into the gaps.

Spelling of scientific vocabulary should be linked to literacy with older learners and links should be made with the technical vocabulary requirements of literacy. The use of a small notebook for the collection of scientific words can be helpful. Better still, if this personal scientific dictionary is then carried by a learner through a key stage it can become very useful for long-term reference. The use of crosswords can be further developed by providing a completed crossword, but without clues. Learners can then be challenged to produce the definitions. These definitions can then also be added to the learners' own scientific dictionaries.

Starting from the answer and developing the question (Figure 9.3) provides learners with the opportunity to think in more detail. For example, provided with the answer 'Space', many questions could be asked, from 'Star Trek calls this the final frontier', to 'Sounds will not travel in this medium' and many more besides. A focus on possible questions can lead to discussion with learners about the quality of and categorisation of the questions asked, for example those that are truly questions, and those responses that are really definitions. This categorisation of questions is a skill that can be developed from this type of activity which links very well to other aspects of question-raising discussed elsewhere in this book. Even teachers have found this to be a challenging activity, but challenge brings rewards and enjoyment for the teacher too!

Removing the common term 'forces' from the centre box (Figure 9.3) provides a good starting point to enable learners to link these ideas together.

All these ideas provide the opportunity for learners to develop their communication skills and their ability to work co-operatively in a group while simultaneously

Find bundles of three!

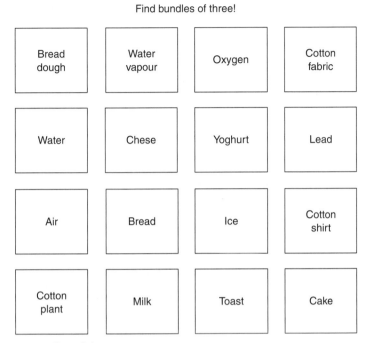

Figure 9.4   Bundles of three

developing their scientific knowledge and understanding. The outcomes from this work can be linked to literacy lessons related to question-raising. These activities can promote thinking by learners and should be encouraged. Thinking skills can also be developed using the 'impossible question' idea; for example, 'What material cannot be washed?' Science and creativity go hand in hand and the teaching skills and ideas used today in primary schools could help pave the way for promoting and encouraging creative thinkers of the future.

Visual Memory Games

Using memory games can enhance visual memory and the ability to make links. The memory is not found in one place in the brain but throughout, and can be enhanced with practice (Ward, 2007). Think of the memory as a muscle, i.e. the more that it is used the better it becomes. 'Kim's game' is a party game played by many learners in the days prior to the video and computer age. Provide the learners with a range of scientific equipment suitable for the topic being studied and allow them to look at the selection for some time. Then remove the items from view and ask the learners to name all the equipment that was provided and give its use. This causes discussions about the types of equipment as well as what they are used for. The development of observation skills is occurring as well as language skills; these functions are situated in different parts of the brain and are being made to work at the same time. Removing only one item could change this activity, requiring the learners to identify what is missing.

Talk about

'Talk about' questions or cards help learners with difficult science concepts or ideas that relate to their everyday lives. They can be used to challenge common misconceptions. Start by providing the learners with a question on the board to spark discussion: 'Why would a scientist think it is strange that your mother tells you to turn the volume on the television down?' or 'What would an unhealthy person do?'

It is also effective to provide a range of true and false statements or ideas about a topic, such as smoking or drugs, to challenge a viewpoint. For example, 'All people who smoke die', 'Smoking makes you slim', 'Smoking makes your teeth go brown', 'Smoking makes you one of the gang'. Learners should debate and evaluate the ideas provided to refine their views and opinions ensuring that they can use evidence to support their views. This is a good starting point for fact and opinion work in other subjects and can stimulate the need to use research skills. It also allows some difficult topics to be discussed by learners without it appearing that the teacher is judging what happens at home.

Games to Help Learners Make Links

Games like 'finding bundles of three' (Figure 9.4) help learners to make links. Making links and identifying why things are part of a pattern are important scientific skills. This type of learning is active and requires the learners to be engaged in their learning. There are a number of threes that are easy to spot and are about where materials come from. The 'finding bundles of three' activity helps to expose misconceptions, for example, some learners are not aware that cotton comes from a plant and in fact suggest that: 'Cotton comes from a cotton wool, it is like a sheep but it does not live here' (Year 2 learner in urban school). The solid, liquid and gas state of water is easy to spot. To provide more of a challenge, learners could be asked to spot other gases or to identify three solids. Learners' talking in science lessons is often an underrated activity that needs a higher profile in many classrooms.

Learners can also make links by playing 'odd one out' (Figure 9.5). It is important to start with a number of real objects with young learners so that the pattern can be found, increasing the number of items with older learners. There is often more than one answer; this is important as it prevents the learners seeing science as a series of questions in which their role is to find out what the teacher is expecting as the answer. Science in real life is not cut and dried and there may be many answers, some of which are not yet known. Use real objects or pictures and words until you are sure the learners' sight vocabulary is developed enough just to provide the words. Learners of different ages and abilities tend to choose different objects as the 'odd one out'. The object chosen by learners of course will depend on their previous knowledge and understanding of the properties of

Figure 9.5   Odd one out

materials. For example, some younger learners may select metal 'because it made the light bounce', whilst most primary-aged learners are likely to select wood 'as the rest will change state'. Metal might be selected 'because it will conduct electricity', and 'because it is magnetic'. An adult learner might select metal, as 'it is not made of more than one type of element', whilst another might suggest metal as the odd one out because 'the rest have carbon in them'.

While games can be made from everyday resources, it is important to ensure that knowledge learnt through games is scientifically correct, as learners will remember both the activity and the learning. It is also important to remember that some questions in science can have more than one answer. This is important and should be encouraged through such discussions, a clearer understanding of the correct meaning of scientific terms can be developed.

While it is possible to teach information by rote, for many learners this will only last in the short-term memory. Learning by rote does not enable the link to previous experiences and the learner makes little sense of the learning. As a result they can know less and be more confused than they were before the lesson.

Five-Minute Science

There are times when it is helpful to provide questions where the learners select the answer from a range of answers provided. Five-minute science is also available in an interactive whiteboard format (TTS, 2007). When selecting questions it is important to include some of the common misconceptions. As the answer to the question 'What are the incisors for?' had some learners suggesting B from the following:

A – to cut the food
B – to stop the food from falling out of the mouth
C – to tear the food
D – to grind the food

Again, it is not just the right answer that is important, but *why* it is the right answer. Questions should be posed about why the learners selected this answer and why the other answers are not right. In mathematics there has been an emphasis on asking learners to explain how they worked out the answer, that the answer itself was not the only outcome of the learning but the strategies adopted for solving the problem were also important. This emphasis is also important in science so that learners are not just asked to learn the right answer and accept ideas without being asked to articulate why they are right. Later in a learner's science education this ability to justify beliefs will be even more important, and fundamentally this is what science is all about. The nature of scientific idea is central to the science programmes of study for learners over the age of 11 and is part of the revised English National Curriculum for Key Stages 3 and 4 (DCSF, 2007). The famous scientists who struggled to develop the immense body of knowledge that is known today had to be able to justify and convince an often-sceptical public that their ideas were correct.

While challenges are an effective learning approach – they relate to the idea of 'hard fun' proposed by Papert (2002) – so is presenting information in different formats to ensure that learners are able to transfer knowledge and understanding from one context into another. The example of a challenge in

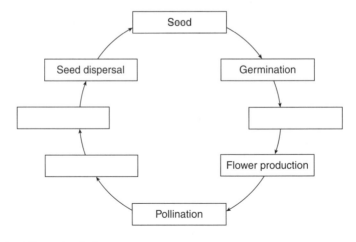

Figure 9.6   Life cycle of plants

Figure 9.6 has gaps that need to be completed. Other cycles in science could also be used to challenge learners' understanding. Just turning the arrows the other way round has dramatic effects with some learners, as does presenting the same information as a linear flow chart. Altering the format of all work is strongly recommended, as learners need to be made to think.

Playing 'twenty questions', another popular game from the past, can provide challenge and help learners to ask effective questions. These are the questions that will identify an object selected by the teacher as quickly as possible. To play 'twenty questions' learners have to ask questions to which the answer can be only 'yes' or 'no', but if they state an object (guess) and it is not the right answer they lose a life. Lives are also lost if the question cannot be one to which the answer is 'yes' or 'no'. After playing this game regularly, and by 'losing lives', learners stop thinking about trying to guess the item, e.g. 'Is it a pencil?' and start to think of key questions that will help in all circumstances, e.g. 'Is it alive?' or 'Does it breathe?' The more experiences the learners have, the more the focus shifts towards scientific words and questions. These skills are vital if learners are really to understand sorting, grouping, and classification, all of which are key scientific skills. They are also used when making dichotomous keys, a skill that some learners find difficult.

Games to Consolidate Learning

Using a beach ball with scientific vocabulary written on the sides provides a quick and easy way of recapping language. The ball is thrown or rolled to a learner who has to explain what the word near their right thumb means or give a definition of the word so that the other learners in the class guess what they are referring to. Other language games include ideas from television programmes including games where the learners have to pass from one side of the board to another answering scientific questions whose initials are identified on the board (Figure 9.7).

There are many commercially produced board games and true/false games, as well as activities that enable learners to act out elements of science. The possibilities are unending. Whilst not all lessons should be game related, elements of the games discussed in this chapter will promote learning and some games-related activities should be built into the science teaching in each topic. The most important criteria as to whether a game should be used at all relates to the learning intention of the lessons. If the learning intention can be met through a game approach, then deciding which game is the next decision, along with knowing what the learners will learn as a result of this game. Games are not the panacea to poor science teaching and should only be used in appropriate amounts to develop skills and understanding. The starter games can have the greatest impact as they get learners motivated to learn, while in the plenary they enable learning to be consolidated. Some games are ideal during the main teaching section of the lesson for groups or specific individuals. However not all science lessons will follow a three-part format and games might occur in the odd five minutes at any time of the day or week.

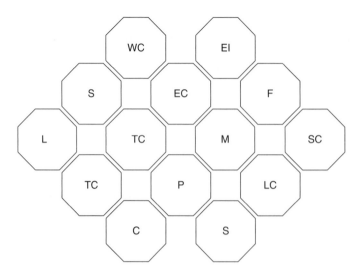

L Where the plant makes its food
What S is used to separate material?
TC A word used to describe a material that will let heat pass easily,
P The name for an organism that preys on others
M The name for materials that are attracted to magnets
F A type of force
What SC is found within a food chain

Figure 9.7   Blockbuster game

Summary

This chapter has shown the positive role games can play within a well-planned scheme of work. Not only can such games be motivating and enjoyable for learners and their teacher, but they can also effectively reinforce important aspects of learning. More specifically, the games presented have been justified in terms of how they can help in the development of scientific vocabulary alongside knowledge and understanding of science. Importantly, the chapter has shown how games can be used to expose and deal with learners' misconceptions.

One important aspect running through this chapter is the importance of learners being provided with regular opportunities for discussion and collaboration. The importance of learners engaging in collaborative work cannot be overemphasised. The learners of today will be growing up to work in a world where, if knowledge is needed, the Internet will provide, but group working and collaboration will be the skills most used on a day-to-day basis.

The final word on games is that there are many still to be invented, modified or rediscovered that will improve science teaching and learners' learning. Enjoy!

Further Reading

Mant, Wilson and Coates (2007) 'The Effect of Increasing Conceptual Challenge in Primary Science Lessons on Pupils' Achievement and Engagement', *International Journal of Science Education*, 29, 14 pp.1707–19.

10

Organisational Issues

Hellen Ward

Introduction

This chapter focuses upon the organisational requirements for science teaching. The organisation of the learners, the equipment and the activities will be discussed as these will affect the learning outcomes provided for the learners. Various groupings and organisations are possible and the ones selected will rely in part on what is to be taught but will also have an impact on the resources available, as well as the confidence and experience of the teacher. Resources and their storage also have an impact upon science teaching and some ideas are suggested. The chapter concludes with issues related to health and safety.

Groupings

The ideal grouping of learners is dependent on the learning outcome expected. If the learners are to learn how to read a thermometer, then the groupings must enable all learners to have access to a thermometer and appropriate media to measure. If the resources allow, this could be accomplished with all learners working independently, but other groupings might enable resources to be more carefully managed and provide opportunities for turn-taking, and enable ideas to be reinforced during group discussion.

As the focus of science teaching is upon learning and not just coverage, the activities provided are as important as the seating arrangements. While it is common practice in coverage models to use 'drill' and worksheets, learners are given greater opportunities to learn about science when they work on interesting activities in pairs or in collaborative groups. Most learners remember more and make a greater number of links when discussing ideas and debating issues. When the ideas and views within the group differ, more discussion occurs and as a result more opportunities for learning are provided. Equipment choices will also impact upon grouping, for example, digital microscopes enable sharing of experiences and lively debate to occur, while manual microscopes can only be operated by one person at a time.

Individual work is appropriate for mind maps, free-range concept maps or for the development of some basic skills. Learners should always be encouraged to record and communicate their own findings with differentiation by resource, support or outcome. This enables all learners to 'download' their experiences, which is needed if links are to be made with previous learning experiences. Downloading, unlike copying off the board, requires some independent thought and participation by the learner.

Paired work is needed for activities requiring more than one pair of hands. Making circuits, dissolving sugars or testing parachutes are difficult activities for lone workers. Working in mixed-ability pairs allows a 'less literate' learner to focus on the task rather than on written recording or the reading of instructions. Most illustrative work can be undertaken in pairs and these activities work poorly with a group of larger numbers due to limited table space and opportunities to access the equipment, with some learners taking the role of bystanders or 'onlookers'.

While pairs are effective in many situations, when equipment and resources are limited or a complete investigation is planned, groups of three are more appropriate. Triads work very well for complete investigations because of the opportunities provided for the learners to take different roles (see Chapter 5).

Groups of four need to be handled carefully, as pairs or a group of three and a 'lone child' can form. Groups of more than four rarely work, unless the focus is on drama or discussion, due to the limited number of roles possible. A larger group of five or six mixed-ability learners is successful for KWHL grids or debating activities as a wider range of ideas is provided. The problem with larger groups is the dominance of a single learner, with others sitting back and watching as there is little for them to do. In primary education the average group size is six, which is too large for most activities that are undertaken, and smaller groups are needed for effective learning. Large groups also have the added disadvantage that all the questions and ideas pass through the teacher with him/her controlling the debate. This issue does not only relate to science teaching and can be overcome by passing a small beach ball/beanbag around the class, allowing only the learner with the ball/bag to present their ideas along with their evidence for these. The ball can only pass between learners, who may have the same or contrasting views. This activity needs to be handled carefully with younger learners, and all learners need to be taught how to debate and discuss their ideas. It also requires the learners to listen to each other and not just wait for the ball/bag in order to state their own idea, so real listening skills are needed.

Although the number of learners in a group is important, the composition in terms of gender and ability also needs thought. Grouping is dependent upon the personalities of the learners, how they interact as a unit, along with the teaching style of the teacher. Friendship groups are often of mixed ability and provide support in some cases and distraction in others. Ability in science is not the same as being numerate or literate and, if Isaac Newton were in school today, he may not have found his way into the top set! Although mixed-ability grouping counteracts this, science ability groups are also needed to enable learners to progress. If the tasks are really literacy tasks lurking in science lessons, then the scientifically able will not be challenged.

For investigative work, mixed-ability, single-gender groups support all learners. When mixed-gender and same-ability learners were placed together the results for the learners, and teachers, were not as effective. The most able learners who were put together argued and could not decide upon a focus, whilst the less able learners demonstrated clear patterns of 'learnt helplessness'. Mixed-ability groups gave peer support. For equal opportunity reasons, single-gender groups give all learners opportunities. In mixed-gender groups the boys collected all the equipment but were then unable/unwilling to work with the girls, who often became the scribes. Grouping is a skill for the teacher who may need to alter the groups until supportive working groups are found. There will also be some learners who find these skills hard and will need to be moved from group to group so that no one group is less successful every time.

While the pattern for investigative work seems clear, it is not for other types of science. With the majority of science being composed of a range of illustrative and basic skills, lessons grouping needs to be flexible, with the composition and size of the group determined from the outcomes of formative assessment.

Organisation

There are many different types of organisation possible for teaching science and all have advantages and disadvantages. Organisation of learning should principally depend upon what is to be learnt. The type and amount of equipment that is available, time allocated, health and safety implications, learners' prior experience of the aspect of science and their group work skills should be considered. Organisation choice should primarily suit the learning needs of the learners but might be selected for real (or perceived) practical constraints.

All organisations are variations on the whole class or small group theme. Whole class organisation (Figure 10.1) is beneficial for introductions to lessons or for lessons where all the learners will be carrying out the same activity at the same time. Whole class is often used when sharing science books, for demonstrations and in the plenary. Small group work is suited to situations when the learners will be working on different activities, whether that is as a circus (see Figure 10.3) or when only one group of learners is carrying out a science activity.

Whole class organisation, working with the class as a unit, does not have to be 'chalk and talk'. It is also beneficial to use a range of artefacts, discussions and pictures at the start of the lesson in a whole class setting. The advantages of whole class organisation are that the learning can take place within a familiar setting, aiming for all the learners to be involved. There is an apparent classroom control and the intention that the learners will be able to share ideas. In a whole class setting there are opportunities to demonstrate particular equipment or aspects of subject knowledge, and control over progression and continuity is provided. However, there are disadvantages if this organisation lasts for the whole of the lesson and is directed from the front with no involvement of learners as individuals. When the whole class is taught as a

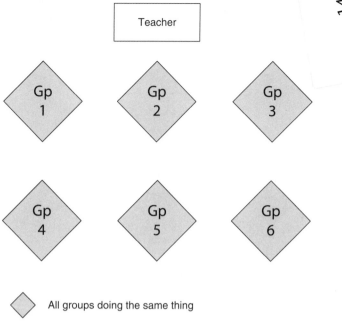

Figure 10.1   Whole class organisation

whole it is difficult to ensure that all the learners listen and are on task and differentiation is only possible by effective questioning. Learners can be relatively passive in their learning, and there is little equipment needed, so the learners will not be given opportunities to develop basic skills.

Setting the same activity for all the groups at the same time, with groups all undertaking the same practical task has an advantage in that learners can be clear about the task set as only one activity is explained. Learners are able to work at their own level, and interest is gained due to the practical nature of the task. The equipment is the same for each group so organisation is simplified and differentiation by outcome or support is possible. In the plenary there are opportunities to share experiences, although this sharing of ideas is limited by the amount of 'new' information to share. Lessons planned in this way can promote progression and continuity, but only for the class as a whole. The disadvantages of this approach are related to differentiation and resources. With all groups undertaking the same activities, matching this to the individuals is difficult and, although the equipment is easy to organise, the demand is high, as each group requires the same equipment. Planning the first lesson in a series using this organisation enables initial assessment of learners but the success of this organisation is dependent upon extension activities and support. Small group independent enquiry, also known as 'child-centred' investigative work (Figure 10.2), enables learners to raise their own questions and carry out the whole process of investigating an idea. The advantages for the learners include motivation, differentiation and the development of group work skills (attitudes). The composition of the small groups enables the needs of individuals

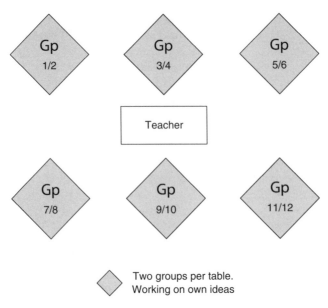

Figure 10.2 Investigative work

to be carefully matched. Thus progression of the learners' own skills is more likely and the opportunity for shared learning is enhanced. The demands for equipment are great and can be complex. Undertaking this organisation requires mental agility and some form of scaffolding for learners. This organisation improves with learner and teacher experience and confidence.

The organisation, known as the 'circus' (Figure 10.3), where learners work on different activities throughout a session, or over a number of sessions, provides many advantages. The learners experience many related activities providing opportunities to develop skills and understanding. Interest is maintained as time on each task is limited and the intense practical nature provides opportunities for group work, skill development and immersion in an aspect of science. 'Circuses', however, do have some key disadvantages. Differentiation is by outcome or support and it is not possible to have progression between the activities provided, as all learners will work around them in a different order. The learners undertake the different activities at the same time, and expectations and outcomes of individuals have to be carefully monitored, particularly for those learners requiring support. Ensuring that all groups finish in time to be moved to the next activity can be problematic. However, with clear instructions and time checks it can be operated successfully. By the very nature of the organisation there are high equipment demands and this can be difficult to arrange. Even with all these issues taken into account, it is a method preferred by many learners, and circuses in the areas of forces, sound and light seem to work successfully.

Thematic group work (Figure 10.4), where all learners are studying science but are not all undertaking a practical science activity, is becoming more popular. This approach is beneficial for the introduction of key skills or ideas and,

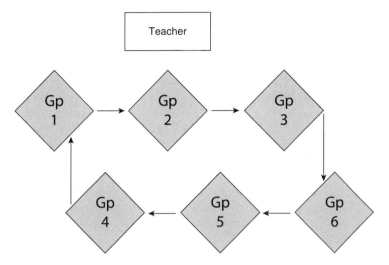

Figure 10.3   The circus

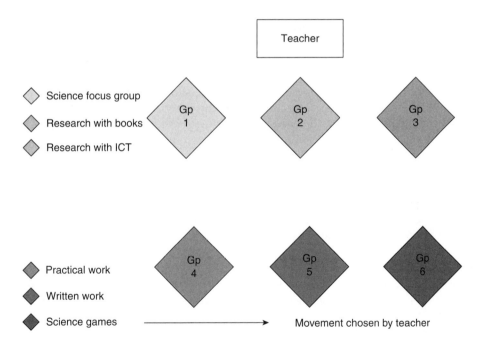

Figure 10.4   Thematic group work

as one group of learners is focused upon, their understanding can be assessed and future learning planned. The focus group offers the opportunity for high quality interaction whilst all the other activities can be set within a context or theme. The disadvantages depend upon the progress made by the learners not in the focus group. These issues have been overcome in literacy and numeracy teaching by making learners more independent in their learning. The key to success is the challenge and quality of the independent activities. Although time-consuming to enable all the learners to experience all the activities, and problematic from a differentiation angle, it is a useful organisational strategy enabling the integration of secondary sources and ICT throughout a unit and supporting situations with limited equipment.

A worryingly common feature of primary science teaching is teacher demonstration with the support of a chosen few learners. There appears to be apparent control over progression and behaviour, and little equipment is needed. Exciting and interesting experiments that learners could not undertake independently can be shown, although, in practice, demonstrations are often of everyday activities that learners are very capable of undertaking independently. The disadvantages of this method far outweigh any advantages, as demonstrations are 'hands off', minds off experiences. Opportunities for differentiation are reduced to teacher questioning, which, when undertaken within a full-class demonstration, often results in low quality recall. Opportunities for learners to develop skills are limited and gaining an insight into learners' attainment is a challenge. However, demonstrations are excellent when carried out by visiting science theatres and groups, as these are one-off exciting events that motivate and inspire.

The science table with an interactive display that challenges learners to undertake practical tasks is an organisation rarely used. The learners visit the table throughout the week in groups (or pairs) engaging in a mixture of child-initiated activities, exploration and illustrative tasks. The activities are controllable and changed weekly to engage and motivate learners. If this method is the only approach to teaching then progression is slow. Assessments are straightforward as few learners undertake the activity at any one time; but teaching time needs to be allocated for this. Time is needed for instruction giving and for a plenary and the timing of these important activities is problematic. Equipment demands are few in terms of quantity, but high in terms of quality and variation of experience provided in a teaching unit. The isolated nature of the activities, with limited opportunity for the learners to share their experiences and the difficulties inherent in planning for individuals, make this a difficult organisational choice. Although more common in Early Years settings, this organisation has value throughout all stages of education if it is provided in addition to other approaches.

Integration (Figure 10.5), where science is one of many tasks available to the learners to select at different times of the day or week, lost favour with the introduction of national primary strategies. Operated effectively in Foundation Stage classrooms, learners select from a range of teacher-directed and child-initiated activities throughout the day and week. The approach enables flexibility of time and resources, differentiation by task, progression and assessment. The focus is clearly centred upon the learner and their learning, and the adult takes a facilitator role. The approach requires some direct input with follow-up activities and resources planned in advance. This method requires very careful planning and accurate record-keeping, ensuring that learners do not produce inadequate work in order to progress quickly to another activity. This factor is not unique to only this organisation but needs careful monitoring. The equipment demands, although very varied, are reduced as only one group is focused upon science at any one time.

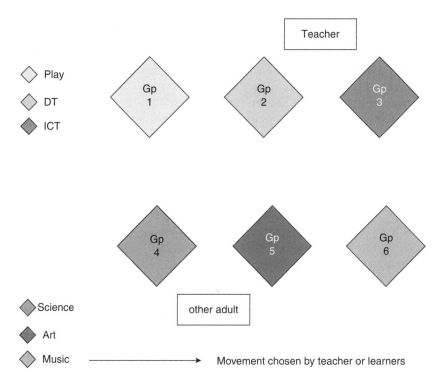

Figure 10.5   Integration

Individual learning programmes are now viable with the development of computer technology. The programmes allow learners to work through levels and experience 'virtual' science activities, with some systems also enabling assessments to be stored. Using this approach it is technically possible to match the activity directly to the needs of the learner, giving complete differentiation, progression and continuity. However, the limited opportunities for sharing ideas, for group work and for the manipulation of real resources and equipment are clear disadvantages. The approach does not develop basic science skills or reinforce the understanding that science activities do not 'always provide the same answer'. Although clean and easy to operate, it somewhat misses the point of what science is. Not all learners learn effectively using the non-linear learning associated with computer-generated activities, and these activities should enhance but not replace traditional practical science. Although very sophisticated, using this new technology may actually only provide an electronic workbook, which is a criticised mode of learning.

Using a range of organisational approaches within science teaching is the most effective way to maintain interest and promote learning. Starting some lessons with a whole class format where learners' ideas are elicited and written up on the board, as the ideas held, is very effective. This can be followed by group practical tasks focused on collecting evidence, followed by a whole class discussion to evaluate the original ideas. At this stage some of the learners' original ideas are no longer viable; they do not have evidence to support them. These are removed, leaving some to be challenged again. This cycle of elicitation of ideas, testing to gain evidence and evaluation might occur more than once in a lesson.

The important thing is to change the style and format of the lesson; too often the three-part lesson imposed by strategies has gravitated to science lessons. Some lessons may last for a morning whilst others might have many small starters, practicals and evaluations contained within them. Lessons using a circus organisation will look very different but it is this difference that will awake learners to learning and perhaps make them more enthusiastic.

Regardless of the organisation method selected, good science teaching should have an opportunity to discuss findings and conclusions; 'hands on' is not successful without some element of 'minds on'. If science is taught in short afternoon sessions, effective elements of science can be lost through tidy-up time. It is important to provide opportunities for learners to explain what they have seen and understood; this occurs in the plenary. Whilst this whole class forum is the favoured option, only using 'show and tell' approaches will not enable learners to develop real understanding. Having a quality conclusion to the lesson requires detailed planning and imagination at the planning stage. Using a range of dance, drama, tape recording or mock television news reports alongside more traditional methods enables the plenary to be more meaningful and enjoyable for the learners. A good plenary enables the next steps of learning to be planned, but need not occur only at the end of the session.

Whilst the focus upon what the learners are to learn is the key factor in organisation selection, previous experience of group work will have an impact upon learning. Learner behaviour, actual or expected, plays a large part in organisational choices. The issue of control is made more difficult by whole class demonstration with limited practical experience, as there is little to motivate the practically orientated learners. However, rushing into group work with full availability of all the equipment is not the answer, as learners will have no experience of how to use this equipment or work with each other. Building up the learners' confidence and discussing expectations, both of ways of working and of outcomes, are needed. Learners who have been too directed lose the ability to think for themselves. Symptomatic of this are the low-level questions learners ask related to 'underlining titles', 'collecting resources' and 'where to write on the page'. However, careful grouping of learners with clear practical activities followed by meaningful recording and discussion enables them to learn science in a controlled and supported way.

·Resources

The management of resources differs from school to school. The decisions taken depend on the amount in the budget, the number of classes and the status of science as a subject in the school. Whilst there is no one way to organise science resources, there seem to be some ways that are more efficient than others. Successful systems generally have the following characteristics:

- The resources have been audited.
- There is an up-to-date resource list including pictures and the number of each item.

- There is a clear storage system with some type of coding.
- There is a method of communicating shortages between teaching staff and the co-ordinator.
- Systems are in place to deal with 'one off' resource issues.
- Storage is arranged both centrally and in the classroom.

Resource Auditing

Identification of the resources as those that are essential (E), desirable (D) and additional (A) is a good starting point. Essential items are investigative equipment in class set quantity, including thermometers, timers, stopwatches, measuring cylinders, scales (preferably digital), magnifying glasses (of various magnifications) force meters and mass carriers. While it is essential to have a range of ICT sensing equipment, some hand-held sensors for light and sounds would be desirable. Digital microscopes and digital cameras in multiples are desirable but having one of each is essential. The judgements will depend upon the school and are subject to change with changing technology and innovations. Although commercially produced games develop vocabulary, these are classed as desirable items only, because they can be made; however, it is more difficult to make working thermometers.

Resourcing science has been a challenge and, with changing national expectations, schools have equipment which is old and unused in addition to new resources that are no longer in the central store. Resource amnesties work effectively.

Storage Systems

Colour coding of the boxes and trays helps with storage and retrieval as does having a picture of the item on the outside of the box alongside its name. Storing all associated equipment in the one area denoted by a one colour tray/box or colour spot also adds order.

Ordering the equipment in associated sections makes more sense than an alphabetical list; for example, resources for measuring distance, resources for measuring forces, resources for work in the environment. Having resource files in each classroom enables learners to select their own equipment and exposes them to associated vocabulary.

As there are no 'fairies' that tidy stock cupboards, storage ideas that are effective at point of use in the classroom are needed. If everything is just piled into a box then there will be chaos, but if equipment is placed in labelled boxes or bags within larger transparent trays or boxes, sorting and tidying begins in the classroom. Devices that enable learners to collect and return their own equipment within the classroom do not have to be complex. In electricity, hanging crocodile clips on wire coat-hangers makes storage easy and enables learners to be responsible for collecting and returning their own equipment. Placing electrical equipment in a large toolbox with each section labelled has made storage, collection and replacement of standard equipment easier to manage. Making appropriate resource choices initially is important, e.g. appropriate voltage bulbs of 3.5 volts,

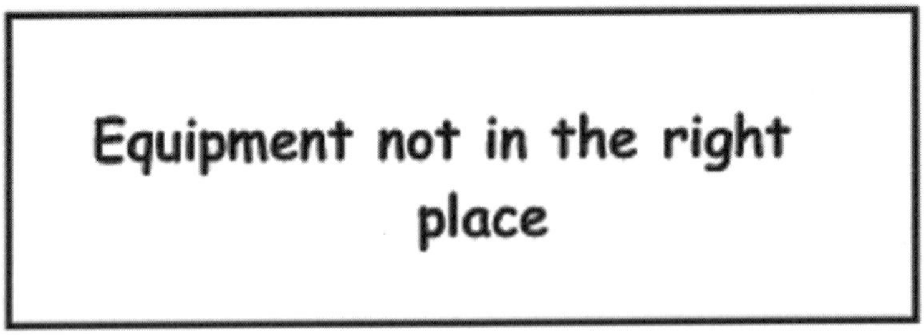

```
Equipment not in the right
          place
```

Figure 10.6   Resource label

rather than 1.5 volts, provides a longer lasting resource with fewer blown bulbs in the classroom. Using 4.5 volt batteries, which stack, rather than 1.5 volt cells enables easy storage and equipment that works when required. When buying from catalogues, if the item is not as expected from the picture, then sending it back is the correct option.

If equipment is not easy to access or replace, this will contribute to non-practical science lessons. However, there will be occasions when equipment turns up after the lesson has finished. This equipment is then left in the class-room, placed somewhere else, or slipped on a shelf between boxes for someone to find later, thus effectively removing the item of equipment from the school stock and denying its use by other teachers and learners. Acknowledging that this is an issue and providing a labelled box (Figure 10.6) to such the equipment into is one solution. Science teaching assistants can replace it in its correct box. The use of science teaching assistants is increasing, with larger schools having more than one. In some schools Year 6 learners are science monitors and sup-port the science leader.

Shortages

Consumable items are as important as hardware and a budget is needed for replacement batteries, bulbs, sugar and food substances throughout the year. All substances including sugar and salt must be labelled, and chemicals which could cause problems if inhaled, ingested or touched should be risk assessed and locked out of harm's way. The common peanut can cause problems for some learners and copper sulphate crystals are poisonous if ingested.

Communication strategies that enable information to be transferred without the need for a face-to-face meeting are ideal, as even with the best systems there will be shortages. How the shortages are dealt with can make the differ-ence between effective and non-effective science teaching. A whiteboard and pen in the science area, for people to write up requests and suggestions, is suc-cessful (tie the pen securely to stop it from walking!), as is sending an evalua-tion sheet to all teachers at the end of the unit of work. However, asking for contributions from colleagues is only successful if action is taken as a result.

With careful planning it is possible to borrow certain large pieces of equip-ment that will only be used once or twice per year. Local secondary schools can help and this provides additional opportunities for cross-phase liaison.

If practical science is to be undertaken regularly, then equipment is vital. Science boxes in each classroom to augment the centrally stored resources are ideal. These can contain a range of items such as magnets, magnifiers, mirrors, torches, tape measures, thermometers, pipettes and syringes. In the Early Years such boxes enable child-initiated activities to occur. At the end of Key Stage 2 the equipment in the class box can include items that would promote additional experiences, for example neon bulbs, for the gifted and talented learners. At all ages the equipment can be tailored to provide interesting and fun activities that link science with their everyday lives. Providing one item of interest for the class each half term is also effective. Resource selection needs to include all teachers, as choice is valuable in all areas of learning and motivation is linked with this. A request list in the staffroom enables ideas to be shared, raises awareness and promotes interest, all of which result in more active science lessons, as teachers are more willing to use equipment and games which they have selected themselves.

Health and Safety

Health and safety comprises two aspects: first, the role of the teacher and, second, the role of the learner. Initially it is expected that learners will follow instructions from the teachers to control the risks to themselves and others. This develops to being able to use equipment and materials appropriately and take action to control the risks.

It is often assumed in primary schools that health and safety is a matter of common sense. The Association of Science publication called *Be Safe* is specifically for primary schools, and was provided by most local authorities for all their schools. It was prepared in consultation with HMI and the Health and Safety Executive. *Be Safe* sets out in a very clear way the main aspects of safety advice and guidance which are needed for teaching both science and technology at Key Stages 1 and 2. The layout includes guidance on activities and resources that are unsafe but also goes on to suggest alternatives to enable good teaching and learning to occur. The other main health and safety body is an organisation called the Consortium of Local Authorities for the Provision of Science Services (CLEAPSS). More than 95 per cent of the education authorities in England, Wales and Northern Ireland are members of this organisation. The function of this body is to support the teaching of practical science through a range of publications and provision of in-service training for teachers and technicians. They run a helpline as well as a web-based service (www.cleapss.org.uk) and they will respond to queries from science co-ordinators.

While common sense generally is a useful starting point, sometimes common sense is not enough, as what is commonly thought to be dangerous, such as the use of the cardboard insides of toilet rolls, may have little risk in real-life situations, whilst objects brought in from a 'pound' shop without the appropriate kite marks could be dangerous when used in the classroom setting. The issue of the cardboard tubes from toilet roll tubes is an interesting one as it is one of the items most teachers state are banned. The suggestion is that children could catch salmonella from the handling of these tubes. Although opinion is divided on the matter, CLEAPSS do not believe that there is any evidence of problems with the use of the rolls, or that learners would be exposed to any higher level of germs than in ordinary day-to-day living.

Science should be fun and interesting for all learners, and recommendations by both safety organisations are that risk assessment should be undertaken, but that 'over caution', making risks out of areas of no risk, will lead to limited practical opportunities for the learners. The use of certain types of batteries for circuit work is often debated. Again it is important for teachers in schools to have an understanding of their local perspectives. In some schools the use of these items is banned. The use of rechargeable batteries is generally not recommended for use in practical circuit work due to the likelihood of them becoming very warm. However, they are perfectly safe for use in Roamers or other equipment where the batteries are sealed from the learners. Small 9v watch batteries are not recommended in school due to the dangers of them being inhaled or ingested, and car batteries are on the 'not recommended' list. Whilst daffodil bulbs are poisonous if eaten, digging them up from the school grounds just in case a learner should eat one is taking things to extremes.

Risk assessments should be carried out by teachers to ensure that they are aware of the risks and hazards associated with everyday activities. All activities should be checked and risk assessed when undertaken for the first time. A simple and working definition of hazards and risks is:

> A *hazard* is a potential source of danger.
> A *risk* is a situation involving the exposure to that danger.

The hazard is the cause of danger, for example, with boiling water the hazard is the scalding that could occur and the risk would depend upon how much danger the learners would be exposed to. If the kettle (only a potential hazard if it is full of boiling water which could scald) is in the staffroom, the exposure to learners in the classroom is non-existent. However, if a kettle or jug of hot water is brought into the classroom, this changes the exposure and, dependent upon the number of supervising adults and the age of the learners, the exposure (risk) might be judged as too high. However, some teachers would risk assess this activity as safe. Hazards can be defined as high, medium or low and in the classroom situation a high hazard is one that will cause long-term damage. Medium hazards could be considered to be those which would be uncomfortable and might need some medical attention, but have no great likelihood of long-term effect. A low hazard is something that has a limited effect. The same ranking is also applied to risks. If the event is likely to happen (high exposure to danger) this would be judged as a high-risk activity, whereas a low-risk activity will be one that in normal everyday occurrence or barring 'an Act of God' would not actually happen. Once the hazards and risks have been identified then a risk assessment can be undertaken. These can be formal or informal depending upon the requirements of the school or Local Authorities. Two examples are given below.

- *Cutting up batteries* The cutting up of batteries is a high hazard activity, with the chemicals inside causing damage to the skin. It is difficult to cut open batteries without cut fingers or hands. As it is difficult to make the risk less than high, this activity is a high hazard and medium to high risk, and should not be undertaken. If learners will benefit from seeing the inside of batteries then local secondary schools have models encased in plastic.

- *Opening fireworks* Obviously a high hazard activity with the dangers of burns and blinding and, ultimately, death. The risk of exposure to danger in the classroom is high, with the electrical equipment in most classrooms being able to generate a spark. Resulting in a risk assessment of high hazard and high risk, again this is not an activity to be undertaken in primary classrooms. This is where common sense does not always prevail, as one teacher used common sense to argue that it was an interesting activity for young children to see and as there were no matches in the classroom there would be no risk of the firework going off.

It is important to take a balanced view with health and safety and to risk assess activities to identify a potential hazard and to evaluate the actual risk of that harm happening, then make decisions based on clear evidence. This evidence may change slightly from year to year with different groups of learners, but fun and interesting activities should be created whilst making sure that health and safety issues are taken into account.

Health and safety assessments are written into many schemes of work. However, if teachers want to undertake more innovative and interesting activities in more creative ways, then all practitioners should be able to risk assess. Whilst caution should be encouraged, real life is waiting outside the safety of schools and this should be taken into account. Banning the use of glass items when glass is found everywhere in everyday life is short sighted. Health and safety education is also about teaching learners to deal with everyday life. If glass is broken outside school then the danger to them could be greater because of the lack of experience and exposure. In classrooms learners will not be involved in the cleaning up of glass and the teacher will know to wrap the glass in newspaper and then to place it in a bag and not in an ordinary classroom bin. Discussing these features with learners helps make them safer in real-life situations.

This second aspect of health and safety, that of teaching learners to identify the hazards and risks, is important. Using an everyday setting to start the process is helpful, and thinking of the hazards related to skateboarding works well. The process starts with a discussion about the hazards (dangers) of skateboarding. These hazards are then graded according to the impact of hazard using a scale of 1 to 3, with 3 being very hazardous and 1 being of limited danger. Skateboarding attached to the bumper of a moving car is a high hazard activity (3) whilst using the skateboard on a play area is safer (1). Learners should be challenged to reduce the exposure to the danger – the risk – i.e. if a helmet is worn then the exposure to the danger is reduced. If a skateboard is used at night on a busy main road the exposure to the danger is increased.

The aim is not to worry learners into thinking that living is a totally unsafe activity; but even cutting paper with a pair of scissors has some risk associated with it, if concentration is lost, if it is done while running around the playground, etc. This enables learners to realise that they have some control and are able to make decisions that have a bearing upon things that happen in their lives. Once learners have an understanding of hazards and risks and how these can be judged, these skills should be transferred to investigative activities. Introducing this from the age of 7, at some point throughout each unit of work, enables learners to meet the requirement of recognising the hazards in living things, materials and physical processes, and to be able to assess risks and take action to reduce risks to themselves and others.

Summary

Effective science teaching requires teachers to use many different organisational types and groupings. Some suggested groupings and organisations have been presented with the advantages and disadvantages for each. There is no one way to teach all lessons and a variety of groupings and organisations is recommended. Changing the format of lessons and grouping has been suggested as a vital way to maintain interest and promote motivation. Health and safety is important, especially as society on the whole is becoming more litigious, but this should not be used as an excuse for boring lessons. If all lessons follow the same format and learners are required to absorb information rather than generate their own ideas and understanding of science, then it will continue to be a subject of little relevance to learners. However, if the emphasis is on the learners and their learning, learners of today may turn into the scientists of tomorrow.

Further Reading

Galton, M., Hargreaves, L., Comber, C., Wall, D. and Pell, A. (1999) *Inside the Primary Classroom Twenty Years On.* London: Routledge.

11

The Use and Abuse of ICT

Hellen Ward

Introduction

Information Control Technology (ICT) has huge potential for supporting learning in science but is often not used effectively for a number of reasons. Teachers are often not aware of available packages or not familiar with the opportunities their use could provide for learning. They may find difficulty in the use of the equipment or with the organisation and management of equipment for learning. This chapter begins with a brief overview of ICT and then looks at the uses and abuses from a classroom perspective. Throughout, the focus will be on the wider teaching issues associated with the use of ICT in the classroom rather than on how ICT equipment can be set up and used. Undoubtedly, practical difficulties arise with the use of ICT equipment which many teachers find frustrating.

Some aspects of ICT such as databases and spreadsheets do not feature here because although programs such as 'flexi tree' are easy to use they are constantly being updated and changed. Specific examples are selected to highlight their innovative nature, ease of use or widespread availability. Details of programs that support writing, such as 'clicker', and are modifications to screens or keyboards for special education needs, are also not discussed as other ICT publications cover these aspects much more effectively. Instead, the focus of this chapter relates to how ICT can be used to help learners learn in science, with links to research and case studies to highlight aspects of current practice.

Background

It was in the early 1970s that the first desk top computer was created and this was aimed at scientists and engineers, not businesses or the public. In the late eighteenth century Charles Babbage created the first machine that worked out calculations, but it was the advent of the Second World War in the twentieth century and the need to break enemy codes that led to developments in design and performance. Exactly who invented the first computer is a question that creates great debate in the ICT world; but it was probably Alan Turing, whose ideas formed the basis for the machines now known as computers.

Computers and Information Communications Technology are a vital part of everyday life. It seems hard to believe that only 60 years ago, computers were new, large and so expensive that not even every university had one. Computers are now found in all schools, they also run washing machines, are found in watches, the remote control and many everyday items. Mobile phones, PSPs geographical positioning software that communicates with handsets which can direct the car, all contain Information Communications Technology (ICT); its applications are so much wider than the laptop with its mouse. Many objects used today have Information Communications Technology within them.

The first computers only had hardware and limited memory, but the invention of software tools, which allow the writing of programs, and programming, meant that the amount of memory space and capabilities increased. Now with the World Wide Web and the Internet, information is available to most children in the developed world 24:7. This puts pressure on teachers, as this technology can provide the answers but science is more involved with the questions. Yet researchers have suggested that ICT can help improve learners' attitudes to science.

> that increasing the amount of practical, investigative work in science, particularly when children are using ICT, had a marked, positive effect on their enjoyment of science. (Murphy, Beggs and Carlisle, 2003, in Murphy, 2003: 18)

Research Evidence

The use of ICT in science has not always been recommended, with some teachers expressing the view that ICT would get in the way and prevent children from thinking. This is a limited view but the computer does need to be used in such a way that it supports good scientific practice. As technology has progressed it has brought with it debates concerning equal opportunities and whether this is about all learners having the same entitlement or whether the demand for equal opportunities is more concerned with all learners having the same outcomes. In a recent survey by the British Educational Communications and Technology Agency (Becta) about ICT use in primary schools, teachers reported that ICT is still more motivating for boys (Becta 2007: 12). Becta is the government technology website and is a key website for all things associated with ICT.

Unlike reading a book, ICT is a non-linear medium and, as multi media becomes even more prevalent, with fast-moving images and sounds, there is a debate about whether this could bombard young brains, changing the very way in which these learners' brains are wired (Greenfield, 2006). However there is too little evidence to support such claims at present.

In an ever more technological age, learners at the start of secondary school need to know what ICT is available for them to use, when to use it and why it would work for this task. In order for learners to be able to do this they need to use a range of ICT within the primary school.

Rules for Using ICT

There are three key rules for using ICT in science, originally developed from ideas presented on the Becta website, www. becta.org.uk (2001):

1. The use of ICT must be in line with good practice in science teaching.
2. It must enable the learners to meet the learning intention.
3. ICT should do something that cannot be achieved without its use or enable it to be achieved more effectively.

These have recently been updated by The Quality Principles for Digital Learning Resources (2006). The newly revised principles contain many important features and include information on each of the following pedagogical issues:

- Inclusion and access
- Learner engagement
- Effective learning
- Assessment to support learning
- Robust summative assessment
- Innovative approaches
- Ease of use
- Match of the curriculum

http://partners.becta.org.uk/index.php?section=sa&catcode=_sa_cs_cf_03.

The revised principles provide further depth and are well worth further examination not possible here. However, the three key rules *do* require further examination here as these should always be considered at the planning stage for science activities:

Key Rule 1: The use of ICT must be in line with good practice in science teaching

The question here is 'What is good science?' Good science prompts learners to think, to be curious, to observe, to take measurements, to look at patterns and trends, to identify issues and to communicate their findings and a host of other skills. If a lesson merely enables learners to watch, passively, something on an interactive whiteboard and does not enable or promote the asking of their own questions or the devising of their own ideas, this is not 'good science' or even good learning. Another poor use of ICT would be to encourage learners to look at small living creatures in the environment and then use the Internet to identify them. Learning would be far more effective if an identification book or a page of animals with pictures prepared by their teacher was taken outside with the learners on the hunt. This would help the identification of animals likely to be found and ensure optimum use of time. There are probably few people reading this who have not spent a terrifying amount of time on the Internet looking for information that they never found!

Another aspect of good science would be to help develop scientific attitudes of co-operation, tolerance of uncertainty and respect for evidence as well as skills of observing, measuring and communicating. Where used effectively, ICT can promote in all learners aspects of 'good' science.

Key Rule 2: It must enable the learners to meet the learning intention

This refers to the science learning intention! It is not expected that learners would be taught to use the hardware or software within the science part of the timetable and the focus of the lesson would be firmly rooted in the science and not the ICT curriculum. Science lessons should not focus on how to use a spreadsheet program to enter collected data, but rather, should provide an opportunity to use and apply relevant skills learned in ICT sessions to move science learning forward. If the majority of a lesson is spent teaching learners how to use the ICT hardware or a software program, then it is not a science lesson but an ICT skill-based lesson; for example, learners need to be introduced to data loggers in ICT prior to using them, so that they can use a data logger in science lessons to take readings. In this way they can focus on relevant observation, such as how quickly the cups of water cool, or look for patterns by using and applying this technology. Here the ICT supports the learners' ability to see what happens to the temperature of the water without having to physically draw the graph themselves, thereby spending more time on the interpretation of the data rather than on manipulating the data itself. In this example, the *learning intention* of the lesson could be 'to be able to identify patterns in data' and the *success criteria* could be:

- to be able to talk about what happened to the temperature using the graph
- to use the words 'degrees Celsius' and 'temperature change' in your answer, and for some learners
- to be able to try and explain the graph these using scientific words.

Essentially, the learning intentions and the success criteria are science based, involve a higher level response from learners and facilitate effective assessment informing subsequent planning at an individual and group level. In this way the ICT facilitates the whole process.

Key Rule 3: ICT should do something that cannot be achieved without its use or enable it to be achieved more effectively

This is the most important principle concerning the use of ICT. If an old-fashioned book is the quickest and most efficient way of finding the information needed, or if the use of pictures on a screen does not enhance learning, then the ICT option should **not** be used. If only one learner is asked to touch the interactive screen whilst the rest of the class passively watches what is happening then the ICT is unlikely to enhance learning. If learners were allowed to write their ideas on 'Post- it' notes while they worked instead of having to type up the work later, then the 'Post- it' would win each time.

Questions related to 'how', 'why' and 'when' to use ICT need to be asked constantly at the planning stage if it is not to be used in science to reinforce existing ICT skills and to fill time. However, if learners are enabled to see why one piece of fabric is more waterproof than another using a digital microscope to look at the structure of the materials, which they would not be able to see without using this hardware, then ICT is adding to the science experience offered. The audience provided by another class of learners who can be contacted by email and can comment upon the results and share their own, makes writing a conclusion and communicating the results more authentic and ICT worthwhile.

These principles should be adhered to whether ICT is used for individual learners, for groups with special educational needs or even by teachers when preparing and using ICT for teaching.

 Case Study 11.1 An abuse of ICT

A Year 5 class were studying changing state. ICT was used to help the learners to use a range of secondary sources to find out about evaporation and condensation in the context of the water cycle.

The science learning objectives

- Most learners to identify and use a range of sources to gather scientific knowledge
- To use scientific terms 'evaporation' and 'condensation' when describing the water cycle.

Learners were introduced to the terms 'evaporation' and 'condensation' through an introductory PowerPoint. While good links were made to a previous lesson where they had melted ice and evaporated water from a cup, learners were still having some problems thinking about what evaporation and condensation were. Next, learners were set to work to find out what evaporation and condensation meant within the context of the water cycle. They were told to use 'Google' and type in the words 'water cycle'. Thirty minutes passed where the learners were actively involved with sites that had information about the water cycle. They made notes to share with the rest of the class later. These were stuck on the board at the front of the room and they labelled a water cycle sheet.

At the end of 30 minutes there were a range of notes on the board and most learners had added evaporation, condensation, precipitation, river and sea on their water cycle sheet. Typical examples of what had been written on the notes included:

'This cycle of water is ultimately linked with energy exchanges among the atmosphere, oceans and land'
'The water cycle has been around longer than the world'
'Surface run off and infiltration are part of the water cycle'.

(Continued)

(Continued)

During the feedback part of the lesson it became apparent that although learners had filled in a picture of the water cycle, they had no greater understanding of what evaporation or condensation were than they had had at the beginning of the lesson. The girls who had written about the energy exchanges said:

'Evaporation is water going up to the sun, the sun passes it to the cloud, the wind comes along and the cloud get heavy and then the water falls out.'

At the end of the lesson one learner explained that:

'Evaporation is when it turns into air. The air particles in the water go into the air and then they are not there any more.'

The lesson ended with the teacher telling the learners:

'You have labelled it on the diagrams, so I do not understand why you do not know what it is.'

Research using the Internet works effectively when parameters are provided. The learners enjoyed using the sites but most were too complex. Precipitation was a word they were exposed to on all sites, along with the term 'the hydrological cycle'. However, at the end of the lesson, when asked by their teacher 'What is the posh name for rain?', Josh helpfully suggested 'dripping' and although a range of other suggestions were given including 'acid' and new words such as 'competitionary', 'partication' and 'I have forgotten'; not one learner was able to use the term correctly.

At the end of the lesson when asked about condensation, one learner said, 'It is where steam turns into something when it turns into something.' Another added, 'It's on the mirror when the steam hits it, it turns back because it dries up and the mirror gets all the drips so it drips with water. I am not sure about evaporation.'

These were not isolated examples and unfortunately were representative of the class as all groups were asked the same question and none was able to give a clear understanding of either term as a result of the lesson.

The Stand Alone or the Computer Suite?

When computer technology began to be introduced into schools, the cost of machines meant that single computers with limited software were placed within some primary classrooms. These stand-alone machines had to be used by the learners in rotation and the simplicity of the software and cost of it meant it was not used excessively. Most learners did not have a computer at home and these early machines were large, slow and cumbersome in comparison to those present in today's classrooms.

With the advent of cheaper machines and the change in expectation of teachers and the curriculum, the number of computers in schools has increased. The ratio of pupils per computer has halved from 12.6 pupils per computer in primary school in 2000 to 6.2 in 2006 (Prior and Hall, 2004). In real terms this means a small primary school of 60 pupils will have fewer than 10 computers while a school with 420 pupils could have almost 70 computers. In order to make the most of these computers, many schools now have placed suites of computers in specially developed rooms so that learners can be taught about the use of programs in one place.

Suites are an advantage for the teaching of ICT, but for the use of ICT to enhance science education they can prove problematic. Computer suites are not ideal places to take water or scientific equipment, due to the nature of the equipment, the space on the computer desk and the layout of the room. In addition to these factors, whether or not the machines are networked to the intranet or whether they have direct access to the Internet, or if they have neither, will impact on what they can be used for.

However, many more applications are being bought by schools that are hand held and allow learners to work inside and outside the classroom. The latest hand-held data loggers have good-size screens, are battery operated and do not have to be linked to a computer. The latest movie cameras are also more practical and have a large screen that helps learners focus their efforts more effectively. There are even mobile phones that work as remote two-way radios that are available for the home corner and that can be used in science so that groups can communicate with each other when undertaking activities outside the classroom.

As a teacher, the management of learners within a suite or with a stand-alone needs careful thought, in the same way that classroom management of learners within practical science lessons needs to be considered. Will all learners be able to see? Which pairs work well together? What grouping will be most helpful? How can equal opportunity issues be addressed? Bearing in mind the research reported by Becta, there may be a need to support girls more. Many of these issues are not science-specific issues, but are important in ensuring that all learners are encouraged to take part both in the science and the ICT.

Categorising ICT Use in Science

ICT can be used effectively to aid learning in a number of ways. Ball (2003) suggested ICT could be seen as

- a tool
- a reference source
- a means of communication
- a means for exploration.

In science, *ICT as a reference source* often requires access to the Internet or using specific CD-ROMs. Downloading information from the Internet will prevent learners being on sites that require high reading ages, do not meet the learning intention or confuse and frustrate them. Making a wiki is one way of sharing information and enabling learners to add to it. Data logging, cameras and microscopes will help learners to *explore,* helping them to develop their ideas and make things happen. Into this category could come simulation software. *Communicating information* can occur using video or podcasts and the use of microphones that have a built-in USB and can record up to four hours of sound and will automatically download into Windows media player, will make podcasting accessible to many more teachers (www. Easi-speak.com). Reviewing learning is the area where ICT could make the biggest impact in the future, with learners being able to see themselves undertaking scientific activities and talk about what they were learning, whether their ideas have changed, as well as developing an understanding of the scientific attitudes involved with group work. It is always handy to be able to categorise ICT in boxes and state that this application is only for reference or only for sharing information, but most applications can be used in more than one way, particularly as the confidence of learners and teachers grows. The classification of the types of ICT will be left up to the practitioners for the rest of this chapter.

There is also the issue of the use of ICT as a teaching rather than learning tool. Another area where the debate should occur is whether ICT should be used to make learning easy. In everyday life learners use ICT to challenge themselves with the next level or the quickest time, and generally they will not get involved in games that have little challenge as there is limited skill and kudos. Perhaps this is something to be borne in mind when using and developing ICT in schools.

The Interactive Whiteboard and Data Projectors

ICT is currently used more frequently for whole class activities in schools than by small groups or pupils working on their own. (Becta, 2007)

It is important to separate the use of ICT as a learning tool and the use of ICT as a teaching tool. The use of interactive whiteboard can make lessons more engaging, but the use is a teaching tool for the lesson rather than a learning tool for the pupils, in the same way that a microscope attached to a whiteboard enhances the opportunities given to the learners, but is not directly impacting on their ICT skills or even enabling them to learn. The levels of ICT used in lessons have risen mainly due to the use of data projectors and interactive whiteboards. And the number of interactive whiteboards in primary schools has risen from 0.7 in 2002 to 8 per school in 2006 (Kitchen, Finch and Sinclair, 2007).

The interactive whiteboard does provide the opportunity to motivate and engage pupils. PowerPoint presentations were novel and interesting when they were first used in continuing professional development and initial teacher training courses from the late 1990s, but over-use of this media had left many jaded. However, learners can use PowerPoint themselves as a way of organising what they know and to develop their own thinking. It can also let learners review what they know and share their ideas in a format with others. The use of the interactive whiteboard (IWB) should be questioned, as its overuse could result in learners passively watching the moving images waiting for their turn to come out and touch the board.

The use of an IWB will not automatically make a bad teaching lesson good. Nor will the injection of an IWB mean that learning is suddenly improved (Duffy, 2006, p.101).

However, IWB, have an important contribution to make to science teaching as using them also allows ideas held by the learners at the start of a project to be saved. Whilst in the past these ideas have often been written on a flip chart, they were often not in a format where they were saved to be looked at again. When written on the IWB they will be in their original state, can be added to, saved and printed off! These are advantages that the flip chart, pen and paper recording cannot compete with. This allows learners to see what they knew at the start and what they know now and can help with evaluating how their ideas have changed. This approach would link well to a constructivist way of teaching, as the learners' ideas would be elicited, recorded and then revisited throughout the topic. This approach would enable learners to examine whether their ideas are supported by evidence gained from the practical work or by using secondary sources. It would help learners to keep re-examining their ideas. In the past one of the key questions about constructivist teaching was that there could be a 'class full of ideas' and a scheme of work which made these rather difficult to deal with. However, if these ideas are stored and returned to at the start of each lesson, using an IWB, it will keep them at the front of the learners' minds and make it easier for the teacher to make links with the ideas and the practical work that is occurring. This is far more useful than if they are uncovered at the start of the topic and then not returned to again.

Although not used extensively, perhaps because of the newer nature of the IWB, saving children's ideas from one year to the next is also possible and this would really help trigger memories that are retained but may need some help to be retrieved. This is particularly helpful as the science curriculum is covered on a seemingly never-ending cycle, for example, forces are covered in Year 1, then 2 then 3 and 4 and again in Year 5. Even subjects like electricity are covered on a two-year rotation. Storing the children's ideas allows them to be revisited along with the pictures of the models that they made at the time.

Saving vocabulary from one lesson to the next and building up a bank of key words is an ideal and very effective use of an IWB, particularly when these words can be used in a number of different ways. In some lessons these words could be used to promote what the learners think about definitions and would make a good link to the use of dictionaries. Many science words can be used to look at the origins of words. The link of learning across the curriculum is vital if learners are not to lose sight of learning as a life-long experience that does not stay in a box called science, but is linked to the real world. Also, because this key vocabulary can be retrieved quickly at the switch of a button, there is no need to have a whole lesson on words and word use and it could be undertaken in the odd ten minutes left over before lunch or at the end of the day. Scientific vocabulary needs to reinforced regularly. Whilst IWBs have many uses, they are becoming one of the more abused aspects of science teaching as it is an area where learners take a passive role, which is very different from their use of ICT outside school (Becta, 2007).

Simulations

By their very nature there are some aspects of science that are difficult to see or experience in a classroom. These have always caused teachers problems. The debate about what investigative work can be undertaken with Earth and beyond has raged for as long as the National Curriculum has been in existence. In fact, Sharp and Grace suggested it is the very non-practical, hands-on nature of subjects like astronomy which means that they were dropped from the primary programme of study (Sharp and Grace, 2004).

Simulations offer an opportunity to try out things that cannot be undertaken in the classroom, which is a major advantage for such programs. To be able to see what happens to the amount of mould or the rate of evaporation when the temperature is increased, are aspects that are enhanced by simulations. If the key rules of ICT are used then these simulation activities will only be effective if they can do something that cannot be done without its use or can be undertaken more effectively. Changing the temperature to see puddles evaporate helps consolidate learning because the real event takes too long; seeing the phase of the moon using a simulation helps learners understand the sequence. Some problems occur with some science lab type experiments where the learners could easily undertake the activity and the simulation does not have enough interactive qualities to engage the learners' brains. For example, simulations of cars on different surfaces add little to the real experience. While it might save getting the equipment out and ensure all data does what is expected, it realistically adds little to the learning experience for most learners. The type of programs that, for example, let butter melt when a button is pressed are also limited, as the graphics of many of the programs are so unlike real life that although the teacher is aware of what is being shown the children are not.

Digital Microscopes

Digital microscopes were sent to all state maintained primary schools for Science Year in 2000, and now most schools have at least one and some have one in each classroom. These microscopes are easy to use and have software that is child-friendly. The microscope plugs into the USB port and the software runs from a CD that comes with the microscope. At less than £100 it is ideal for everyday use in the classroom. The fact that the microscope allows learners to see images on a screen without having to try and squint down a traditional eye piece makes them friendly for even the youngest learners. Their use fulfils the three key rules of ICT, as they can easily support good science, they can be used to support the learning intention and they are better than the majority of microscopes used in primary schools prior to their introduction. Objects can be magnified either 10, 60 or 200 times and the choice of movie, still or time-lapse options extends the use of these microscopes. The additional features such as image alteration, making and playing a slide show and the option to download images to other programs, such as PowerPoint or Word, enables these microscopes to support active learning in science.

The time lapse option allows pictures of mould growing on bread to be taken over time and then played back to learners. This allows things that happen over weekends or more slowly to be seen in a time span that is more meaningful to learners. The time lapse has been used to show evaporation of water in different settings, for example, a piece of apple was recorded over a weekend. Another suggestion is using mung beans to show germination.

Issues of pedagogy arise when ICT is introduced; however, good practice in science should be the deciding feature – groups of learners using the microscope and then showing others their slide show is always a more effective learning option than one machine dominated by the teacher and used to show the learners something. It could be that the introduction to the microscope itself might occur as a whole class instruction, but by the very nature of the equipment it is more successful to train one small group who will peer tutor the rest of the class.

Learners left with pond life and a microscope can observe how the larvae moves and that the larvae will not stay in the light. The way these animals move fascinates learners who will then begin to raise their own questions and this observation time can provide starting points for further investigative work. More use of the download option and transferring pictures to other programs would enable a greater use for these images to support all aspects of science.

Data Logging Equipment

Data logging can provide learners with results in graphical form without the need to draw the graph. The data logger does not forget to take readings during playtime and can be set to record from seconds to days. Recent modifications to data logging equipment have seen a new set of equipment that can work away from the computer. These hand-held units have a screen and are portable. They can be re-attached to the computer and the data can then be downloaded. They also work attached to the computer and fed through a data projector so that all the class can be aware of the amount of noise they are making. Data loggers can be used to take readings of sound, light and temperature with inbuilt and detachable sensors. Most systems offer the opportunity to record a heart beat, although many heart rate sensors are expensive and work inefficiently.

Digital Cameras and Digital Films

An effective use of the digital camera is to enable learners to discuss their own work, or themselves working. While many classrooms have digital cameras, teachers often stick pictures of learners undertaking activities in the children's science books as evidence that science occurred. Another approach is to use these pictures of the learners as a starting point for discussion about what they were learning, what issues the learners came up with and how or what they would do differently next time. In the same way that pictures of events in real life are reminders of who was there and events that otherwise would be forgotten, using pictures to stimulate conversions and memories is helpful in science. Another effective use of digital cameras is take pictures of the equipment the children will use and make them into a set of sticky labels (Ward, 2007) this helps less literate children with recording.

Case Study 11.2

Children in one primary school in Kent were given a Christmas challenge to see if they could keep Mr Frosty from melting. This task was one commonly used by teachers, but as the children decided what they would change and how they would find out how to keep Mr Frosty for the longest time, the teacher took pictures of the children working in groups. These pictures were then used with the learners afterwards to ascertain what they had been thinking at the time. Showing the pictures enabled memories and experiences to be discussed and helped with evaluation. Questions were posed about the ways of working in the group and whether their group had co-operated, to find out what had been successful and what they would do differently if the investigation was repeated.

- T;   Could you tell me what the photo is about?
- C1:   I it's when we did our science experiment on how much ice would melt if you insulate it.
- C2:   In the picture we put thick wool about the cup to insulate it.
- C3:   We were finding out how much ice would melt outside and on the radiator, and in the classroom.
- T: What were you changing?
- C1:   We were changing the location of the cup.
- T: What did you find out?
- C3:   We learnt that the outside is... .
- C2:   That it melted outside slower because it is colder, inside it was hotter.
- T: Did you find it helpful to see the photograph?
- C1:   It is probably easier with the photograph because we can see it.
- T: How would you rate the activity.
- C1:   9/10.
- C2:   9/10.
- C3:   9/10.
- T: What would it need to get a 10?
- C1:   To get a ten we would need more time because we did not get much time if you think about it!

(The activity started at 9.30 in the morning and stopped at 2.30 in the afternoon.)

Figure 11.1   Picture and transcript of snowman working (Year 6)

Voice Recording Materials

Tape recorders have been used in classrooms since the 1950s. Taped sounds have been used to help with identification of sounds and their sources, and sound bingo has been popular for some time. Children have also had opportunities to use tape recording to make news reports, reporting their science work to others. Tape recorders have been used to find out what learners talk about in science when undertaking investigative work in groups for assessment purposes. The more current use of recording in classrooms is related to some technology called 'Talk time'. Talking postcards allow teachers and learners to select items and record a message that can be listened to later. A4 size whiteboards with Talk time technology allow learners to record both orally and by writing their thoughts. This can be helpful as a starter, to elicit ideas or as an opportunity to practise skills such as explanations. It can be used over and over again. Using talk time tins on wall displays supports language development.

One of the fun new uses of Talk time technology is 'Chatterstrips', where there are opportunities to record up to 24 pieces of separate information. These can be linked to displays where they can provide information about aspects of the display, ask learners questions or provide prompts for thinking. One excellent display on sound had a set of questions aimed at making the learners think. Some questions challenged misconceptions, some were extension questions and some were aimed at making learners think about the language they use. Examples of questions used included 'Will sound travel in water?' 'How many sources of sound can you name?', 'What is the difference between pitch and loudness?', 'Why would scientists not use the term "volume" when talking about sound?' 'Is there sound in Space?'

As with all technology it works most effectively if the learners are encouraged to interact with it, to take ownership of using it and are allowed then to make their own choices. Abuse occurs when all the recordings made by the learners have to be saved as evidence or where the learners are not instrumental in deciding what they get to keep and what they can change. Talk time postcards are effective when asking children to record their understanding of key concepts such as evaporation, gravity, etc. Allowing them to define these terms, listen to their explanation, make notes on the whiteboard and re-record until they are happy with their responses, enables real learning to occur.

The talking scrapbooks have been an excellent development from Talk time technology where an A3 file has Talk time technology within it and children can add a commentary upon their work. This has enabled floor books to be used effectively with older learners.

Case Study 11.2

The children were investigating which was the brightest torch. They were able to have their ideas scribed and they recorded their ideas in drawings and their pictures were taken. These were then turned into a floor book and the children were able to add a commentary about the activity using the recording opportunity at the bottom of the book.

Online Scrap Book

Many science exercise books from children of very different abilities contain very similar work within them. In part this is because of the perceived need for evidence for accountability purposes, that science has taken place. The outcome is that few learners are learning how to write in science, and explanation and evaluation are the weakest aspects of scientific communication. Instead of having an accountability agenda, it is important that recording occurs in a range of ways and that language development is linked to the way learners learn. ICT can help this by being used to support the development of an online scrapbook. Selecting a couple of learners in each session to have their work recorded digitally provides a wonderful resource for parents, learners and other teachers as well as advisers and inspectors who might visit schools. Work can be included, by taking pictures of what the learners are doing and recording a voice or having a typed transcript alongside. This can bring science lessons to life, provide an opportunity to show a value for the recording, give all learners the chance to shine as well as provide a record of 'science in our class'. It also enables a range of re-coding opportunities to be provided. In Figure 11.2 is an example of 'Parts of the flowers' activity. A greater range of opportunities are provided by schools who have online scrapbooks as they are freed up to think creatively rather than thinking of 'flat things that can go into books'.

Figure 11.2 Flower pictures showing the key parts of the flower

Multimedia Recording of Nature and Change

While the 1978 primary school report was scathing about science in primary schools, children at this time were often given opportunities to observe nature. This link to the environment is important and can encourage important citizenship and 'wellbeing' issues. Taking pictures and making observations of trees, plants and the local environment during the year enables learners to have opportunities to look again at the often imperceptible changes that occur throughout the year. These can be added to the scrapbook and because ICT is more flexible than a handwritten document the learners can place all their observations and measurements about the changes in the environment in pages that can be linked together. Adding multi-media to the scrapbooks can start to make a linear scrapbook more complex. The learners can access text, clip art, voice, still pictures and movie clips of the changing environment at a later time.

Visits from mums and small babies enable the children to ask about what the baby needs and this prompts them to think about how they have changed and grown themselves. Recording these and subsequent visits, with taped interviews, will provide a resource for learning about change. Safe working and access to pictures and videos does need careful thought but looking back at this can provide a valuable resource as well as a visual way to support the learners' memories.

Daylight length is another change that occurs and while learners are often given opportunities to draw shadows at different times of the day, these are often one-off occurrences that are problematic due to atmospheric conditions (it is never sunny for the whole day whenever this lesson is planned). If however a set of measurements and pictures taken over a number of years are digitally stored then learners have a bank of evidence to draw upon. Teachers can use pictures, recording and children's own explanations as a resource bank to help promote future learning.

Even classroom pets can be recorded over time to show how they grow and change; Giant African snails are always popular pets for learners to watch, investigate and explore. A student recently was mesmerised by hearing a snail eat, whilst she was holding the snail on her hand and feeding it cucumber. That fact that the snail was not a quiet eater added to the awe of the experience. Butterfly eggs changing into caterpillars which turn into chrysalises and then butterflies are memories that can be recorded via pictures and words in a school science online scrapbook. These experiences stay with learners and are often the thing they remember when asked to provide a memory of something they enjoyed at primary school.

Summary

ICT is here to stay and the changes and additional technology will continue to enhance the way learners experience the world. While it is easy to bemoan the lack of pedagogical thought given to the introduction of ICT, it is not just ICT that has these issues, as there is little of pedagogical value in a photocopied

(Continued)

(Continued)

worksheet! As the equipment becomes smaller, more user-friendly and the amount of technology in everyday life continues to expand, teachers will continue to use what is effective and what is available within their schools. Primary teachers face continuing issues in ensuring adequate technical support, with a member of teaching staff providing the main technical support in 27 per cent of cases (Becta, 2007, p.14). However, learners outside school learn much ICT-related technology by trial and error, are not put off by 'hard' things and teachers learning alongside the children can be better than not bringing the equipment into the lessons. The main abuse of ICT occurs when it is used as a whole class, minds off, hands off, 'moving pictures' experience that may not motivate or enhance learning.

In the Harnessing Technology Review 2007, Becta stated:

> Whatever the reasons, the use of technology to support curriculum-based learning in schools often gives learners a passive role, representing a very different position from learners' use of technology outside education. The pedagogical approach most commonly adopted is unlikely to encourage the range of competencies increasingly demanded by employers and the economy more generally. It also potentially presents a risk of further dislocation between learners' informal experiences at home and those in education, possibly at the expense of learners' enthusiasm for educational experiences. This is at a time when personalisation debates increasingly recognise the need for closer links between formal and informal learning. (Becta, 2007,1 p.7)

Further Reading

Meadow, J. (2004) *Science and ICT in the primary school: a creative approach to big ideas.* London: David Fulton.

Murphy, C. (2003) Literature Review in Primary Science and ICT Report 5: Future lab. www.futurelab.org.uk/research/lit_reviews.htm

Skinner, N.C. and Preece, F.W. (2003) 'The Use of Information technology to support the teaching of science in primary schools', *International Journal of science Education* 25(2), 205–19.

Wilson, E., Warwick, P., Winterbottom, M. (2006) *Teaching Primary Science with ICT.* Milton Keynes: Open University Press.

Glossary of Terms

In order to ensure consistency of use of terms within the book and also to ensure that the book is read with understanding the following terms are defined.

Basic skills: these are the science process skills that include observation, and other skills that start with simple comparisons that later lead to standard units of measurement, for example, measuring temperature first by comparing samples by touch and later using a thermometer.

Children: will be used when there is a wider issue under discussion.

Experiments: these are scientific procedures designed to demonstrate a known fact in the classroom. Experiments are used to prove what is happening in a practical situation. These are often misused in primary education.

Exploration: where learners are given the opportunity to explore (play with) objects in their environment. Exploration is considered to be an important aspect of learning for most people at all stages of education and beyond. Therefore it relates to the whole school age range and adults. The purpose of exploration is to allow time for observation and for learners to become familiar with objects and to raise questions about the object. This is important both for skill development and the development of understanding.

Exploratory skills: these are the skills developed during exploratory work. These include observation, questioning, pattern seeking, causal relationships (i.e. cause and effect), comparisons and use of vocabulary to describe and explain.

Illustrative work: here, provided practical work may include factors to vary and change, but the teacher makes the choice of these. Learners have no choice. These types of practical work are vitally important because they provide the opportunity for learners to learn important skills or procedures and also provide the opportunity for the practical work to illustrate some aspect of knowledge of science.

Investigations: these provide learners with the opportunity to undertake complete or whole investigations where there are identifiable opportunities to:
- identify factors and change variables
- identify factors or variables to measure or observe
- allow choice by learners.

Learners: will be used throughout to describe children in the context of teaching.

Learning intention: the aim of the lesson. This is what the learners are to learn and should include knowledge, understanding, skills and procedures and attitudes in science.

Learning objective: what learners will do in the lesson.

Learning outcomes: specifically what learners are expected to learn in the lesson. These are used for assessment purposes and differentiated for different groups/individual learners.

Practical work: learners being provided with the opportunity to have 'hands on' practical experiences.

These fall into a number of categories:

1. Investigations
2. Illustrative activities
3. Experiments
4. Basic skills
5. Observations.

Programme of Study: from the National Curriculum and *Curriculum Guidance for the Early Years Foundation Stage.*

Scheme of work: often termed 'medium-term plan'.

Scientific enquiry: an umbrella term that encompasses many aspects of activity. National Curriculum (2000) denotes scientific enquiry as planning, obtaining and using evidence along with an understanding of the nature of scientific ideas. Exploration, illustrative and investigative activities would fall into this.

Scientific process: process and procedures used consistently when learners are engaged in aspects of scientific enquiry.

Structured play: where a situation is set up by the teacher and where the teacher or classroom assistant or other adult asks focused questions to meet planned previously identified possible learning outcomes. There is a flexibility of approach where identified objectives may or may not be met in the session. At the end of the activity the teacher/other assesses what learning has taken place against possible learning outcomes and records these with any collected evidence to support the conclusions reached.

Unstructured play: where the teacher or other adult provides equipment, but there is no clear outcome intended. The role of the teacher here is to stand back from the activity and watch for more informal opportunities to take learning on from a child-initiated starting point. Learning is assessed on an individual basis.

References

Ashby, J. (2007), *General Teaching Council for England Survey of Teachers 2004-06 Report on trend data.* General Teaching Council for England. http://www.gtce.org.uk/ shared/contentlibs/126795/93128/126346/207305/ trend_rpt.pdf

Assessment Reform Group (ARG) (1999) *Assessment for Learning: Beyond the Black Box.* Cambridge: University of Cambridge, School of Education. http://www.assessment-reform-group.org.uk

Assessment Reform Group (ARG) (2002) *Testing and Motivation.* Cambridge: University of Cambridge, School of Education.

ASE (2001) *Be Safe.* Hatfield: Association for Science Education.

Becta (2006a) *Harnessing Technology – Delivery Plan.* Coventry: Becta http:// publications. becta.org.uk/display.cfm?resID=28223&page=1835

Becta (2006b) *The ICT and e-learning in FE Survey 2006.* Coventry: Becta.

Becta (2007) *Management, learning and improvement. A report on the further education sector's engagement with technology.* Coventry: Becta

Black, P. and Wiliam, D. (1998) *Inside the Black Box: Raising Standards through Classroom Assessment.* London: King's College School of Education.

Bruner, J. and Haste, H. (1993) *Making Sense – the Child's Construction of the World.* London: Routledge.

Butt, S. and Cebulla, A. (2006) *E-maturity and school performance – A secondary analysis of COL evaluation data.* London: National Centre for Social Research.

Butzow, C.M. and Butzow, J.W. (2000) *Science Through Children's Literature* (2nd edn). Green wood Press.

Camp, L. and Ross, T. (2000) *Why: Meet Lily, the Little Girl Who Always Asks Why.* London: Picture Lion.

Clarke, S. (2001) *Unlocking Formative Assessment.* London: Hodder & Stoughton.

Clarke, S. (2003) *Enriching Feedback in the Primary Classroom.* London: Hodder & Stoughton.

Department for Education and Employment (DfEE) (1999) *National Curriculum: Science.* London: DfEE.

Department for Education and Skills (DfES) (2003a) *The Education National Curriculum: Foundation Stage Early Learning Goals (England).* (Statutory Instrument 2003, No. 391). London: DfES.

Department for Education and Skills (DfES) (2003b) *Excellence and Enjoyment. A Strategy for Primary Schools.* London: DfES.

Department for Education and Skills (DfES) (2006) *The Science, Technology, Engineering and Mathemetics (STEM) Report.* London: DfES.

Department for Education and Skills (DfES) (2007) Computer: pupil ratios from PLASC 2006. London: DfES. http://www. teachernet.gov.uk/wholeschool/ictis/facts/

Digby, A. and Searby, P. (1981) *Children, School and Society in Nineteenth-Century England.* London: The Macmillan Press Ltd.

Dweck, C.S. (1999) *Self Theories: Their Role in Motivation, Personality and Development.* Philadelphia, PA: Taylor and Francis.

Empirica (2006) *Benchmarking Access and Use of ICT in European Schools.* http://ec.europa. eu/information_society/eeurope/i2010/docs/studies/final_report_3.pdf

European Commission (2006) *Benchmarking access and use of ICT in European schools 2006: Final report from Head Teacher and Classroom Teacher surveys in 27 European countries.* Bonn: European Commission. http://europa.eu.int/information_society/ eeurope/i2010/docs/studies/final_report_3.pdf

Foreman, J. (2002) 'An investigation into the impact of role play on children's attitudes and learning in primary science lessons'. Unpublished MA (Ed) dissertation, Canterbury Christ Church University College.

Gardner, H. (1993) *Multiple Intelligences.* New York: Basic Books.

Goldsworthy, A. (1997) *Making Sense of Primary Science Investigations.* Hatfield: Association for Science Education.

Harlen, W. (1978) 'Does Content Matter in Primary Science?', *School Science Review,* 59, (209), 614–25.

Harlen, W. (2000a) *The Teaching of Science in Primary Schools* (3rd edn). London: David Fulton.

Harlen, W. (2000b) *Teaching Learning and Assessing Science 5–12* (3rd edn). London: Paul Chapman Publishing.

Harrison, C., Comber, C., Fisher, T., Haw, K., Lewin, C., Lunzer, E., McFarlane, A., Mavers, D., Scrimshaw, P., Somekh, B. and Watling, R. (2002) *The Impact of Information and Communications Technology on Pupil Learning and Attainment: A Report to the DfES.* London: DfES

Johnson, G. (1999) 'Kidney role-plays', *School Science Review,* 80: 93–7.

Johnson, J. (2005) *Early Explorations in Science* (2nd edn). Buckingham: Open University Press.

Khan, B.Z. and Sokoloff, K. (2007) *The Evolution of Useful Knowledge: Great Inventors, Science and Technology in British Economic Development, 1750–1930* www.ehs.org.uk/ ehs/conference2007/Assets/KhanIIΛ.doc

Kitchen, S., Finch, S and Sinclair, R. (2007) *Harnessing Technology schools survey 2007.* Coventry: Becta. http://partners.becta.org.uk/index.php?section=rh&catcode=_re_ rp_02&rid=14110

Kolb, D.A. (1984) *Experiential Learning: Experience as the Source of Learning and Development.* Englewood Cliffs, NJ: Prentice-Hall.

Lawson, J. and Silver, H. (1973) *A Social History of Education in England.* London: Methuen and Co Ltd.

Mendelsohn, R. (2006) *Is there a case for aggressive, near-term mitigation of greenhouse gases?* Accessed from http://www.cato.org/pubs/regulation/regv29n4/v29n4-5.pdf on 18/12/07

Murphy. C. (2003) *Literature Review in Primary Science and ICT Report 5: Future lab.* www.futurelab.org.uk/research/lit_reviews.htm

Office for Standards in Education/Her Majesty's Inspectorate (OfSTED/HMI) (2002) *Ofsted Subject Reports 2000–01.* London: HMI. www.ofsted.gov.uk

Office for Standards in Education/Her Majesty's Inspectorate (OfSTED/HMI) (2003) *Ofsted Subject Reports 2001–02.* London: HMI. www.ofsted.gov.uk

Office for Standards in Education/Her Majesty's Inspectorate (OfSTED/HMI) (2004) *Ofsted Subject Reports 2002–03.* London: HMI. www.ofsted.gov.uk

Parliamentary Office of Science and Technology (POST) (2003) *Post Note Primary Science.* September. London: POST.

Pollard, A. and Triggs, P. (2000) *What Pupils Say: Changing Policy Practice and Experience.* London: Continuum.

Prior, G. and Hall, L. (2004) *ICT in Schools Survey 2004,* ICT in Schools Research and Evaluation Series No. 22. Coventry/London:Becta/DfES http://www.becta.org.uk/page_documents/research/ict_in_schools_survey_2004.pdf

Qualifications and Curriculum Authority (QCA) (1998) *Schemes of Work.* London: QCA.

Qualifications and Curriculum Authority (QCA) (2000) *Curriculum Guidance for the Foundation Stage.* London: QCA.

Qualifications and Curriculum Authority (QCA) (2004) *Standards at Key Stage 2 English, Mathematics and Science 2003.* London: QCA.

Qualter, A. (1996) *Exploring Primary Science and Technology: Differentiated Primary Science.* Buckingham: Open University Press.

Roderick, G. and Stephens, M. (1981) *Where did we go wrong? Industrial Performance, Education and the Economy in Victorian Britain.* Lewes: The Falmer Press.

Science and Technology Committee (2002) *Science Education from 14 to 19.* London: House of Commons/Stationery Office.

Science, Technology, Engineering and Mathematics (STEM) Programme Report (2006). DfES/DTI: London.

Sherrington, R. (1998) *ASE Guide to Primary Science.* Cheltenham: Stanley Thornes.

Smith, A. (1999) *Accelerated Learning in Practice.* Stafford: Network Educational Press.

Smith, R. and Peacock, G. (1995) *Investigation and Progression in Science.* London: Hodder & Stoughton.

Somekh, B., Underwood, J., Convery, A., Dillon, G., Jarvis, J., Lewin, C., Mavers, D., Saxon, D., Sing, S., Steadman, S., Twining, P. and Woodrow, D. (2007), *Evaluation of the ICT Test Bed Project Final Report.* Coventry: Becta. http://www.evaluation.icttestbed.org.uk/files/test_bed_evaluation_report_2006.pdf

Taylor, A. (1997) 'Learning science through creative activities', *School Science Review,* 79, 39–46.

Tol, R. (2006) *The Stern Review of Climate Change: a comment*

Van Ments, M. (1983) *The Effective Use of Role Play: A Handbook for Teachers and Trainers.* Revised edition. London and New York: Kogan Page.

Wiliam. D (2003) 'Improving national assessment'. Presentation at the KSA; London, UK. June.

Index